The Kids Book of
GREAT
CANADIAN
WOMEN

WRITTEN BY

Elizabeth MacLeod

ILLUSTRATED BY

John Mantha

KIDS CAN PRESS

Dedication

For Madeleine Paterson-Watt, our Madi, whose 15 years of greatness are measured by her unwavering loyalty to and intense love for her friends and family, her unquenchable curiosity and big dreams, her breathlessness about life and all its possibilities, her hope in the midst of cancer. She made living look so easy. Oh, how she is missed. She was, and is, such light. — bob & MJ & Zoe & Genevieve

Acknowledgements

Many great Canadian women — and men — helped in the research and creation of this book. Thanks very much to you all. I'm especially grateful to James and Mary Lou Foster, genealogists; Alix McEwen, Reference Archivist, Library and Archives Canada; Ann ten Cate, Archivist, British Columbia Archives; Marilyn Belch Venner; David Wistow, Art Gallery of Ontario; Manitoba Archives; Royal Canadian Mounted Police, Historical Office; Saskatchewan Medical Association; and librarians at the Northern District Branch and Toronto Reference Library of the Toronto Public Library.

As usual, John Mantha has created wonderful portraits that really bring these women to life. Designer Julia Naimska has beautifully combined those portraits with the text. Once again, Val Wyatt has amazed me with her editorial skill, attention to detail, patience and good humour. I also appreciate the contributions of art director Marie Bartholomew, photo researcher Patricia Buckley, copyeditor Larry MacDonald and editor Chris McClymont. Thanks to everyone at Kids Can Press for giving me this opportunity to reinforce my pride in Canada and its women. Thank you always to Dad, John and Douglas. Much love to Paul, my favourite great Canadian man.

Many sources have been used for the information in this book but the primary sources are *The Canadian Encyclopedia* and *The Junior Encyclopedia of Canada*.

Photo Credits

Abbreviations
t = top; b = bottom

All stamps © Canada Post Corporation. Reproduced with permission.

p. 7: © 1992 Canada Post; **p. 8:** © 1973 Canada Post; **p. 12:** the *Provincial Freeman* from the Archives of Ontario N40, reel 1; **p. 16:** (t) © 1993 Canada Post; (b) © 1997 Canada Post; **p. 22:** © 1980 Canada Post; **p. 24:** © 2003 Canada Post; **p. 34:** © 2000 Canada Post; **p. 37:** © 1981 Canada Post; **p. 42:** © 1961 Canada Post; **p. 45:** © 1996 Canada Post; **p. 47:** © 1990 Canada Post; **p. 49:** © 1985 Canada Post; **p. 50:** © 1994 Canada Post; **p. 54:** © 1996 Canada Post; **p. 58:** © 1986 Canada Post; **p. 61:** © 2000 Canada Post

Kids Can Press acknowledges the financial support of the Government of Ontario, through the Ontario Media Development Corporation's Ontario Book Initiative; the Ontario Arts Council; the Canada Council for the Arts; and the Government of Canada, through the BPIDP, for our publishing activity.

Published in Canada by	Published in the U.S. by
Kids Can Press Ltd.	Kids Can Press Ltd.
29 Birch Avenue	2250 Military Road
Toronto, ON M4V 1E2	Tonawanda, NY 14150

www.kidscanpress.com

Edited by Valerie Wyatt
Designed by Julia Naimska
Printed and bound in China

This book is smyth sewn casebound.

CM 06 0 9 8 7 6 5 4 3 2 1

Library and Archives Canada Cataloguing in Publication

MacLeod, Elizabeth
The kids book of great Canadian women / written by Elizabeth MacLeod ;
illustrated by John Mantha.

(index included)
ISBN-13: 978-1-55337-820-4 (bound)
ISBN-10: 1-55337-820-2 (bound)

1. Women—Canada—Biography—Juvenile literature. 2. Canada—Biography—Juvenile literature. I. Mantha, John II. Title.

FC26.W6M33 2005   j920.72'0971   C2005-904233-8

Kids Can Press is a *l'°rus*™ Entertainment company

CONTENTS

CANADIAN WOMEN ARE GREAT!

E very March, Canada celebrates International Women's Week. What a terrific opportunity to remind all Canadians of the women who have made big contributions to our country! In this book you'll meet more than 130 great Canadian women and read about their remarkable accomplishments.

You've probably heard of many of the women in this book. Laura Secord (page 7) helped defend Canada during the War of 1812, and Roberta Bondar (page 24) became our first woman in space. But other Canadian women have received little recognition. Dr. Leonora King (page 38) is largely unknown, although she saved thousands of lives as the first Canadian doctor in China. Elsie MacGill (page 17) is mostly forgotten as Canada's first woman aircraft designer.

Many of the women in this book have had to show great determination and courage to get ahead. The first women to attend Canadian universities, including Emily Stowe (page 37), faced name calling and put-downs from male students and professors. Early woman politicians, such as Agnes Macphail (page 47), were frustrated that reporters cared more about their clothes than their opinions on Canadian policy.

Some great Canadian women were lucky enough to have a mentor to help them overcome a challenge or break into a new area of endeavour. Many in turn help other women. For instance, Supreme Court Justice Rosalie Abella (page 58) encourages women to get involved in law. Painters such as Helen McNicoll (page 30) and Paraskeva Clark (page 33) worked in groups of women who supported each other.

Some Canadian women artists, performers and writers have helped bring Canadian culture to the world and have become international stars. Others, such as mountain climber Phyllis Munday (page 25), found adventure within Canada and have made us more aware of what a wonderful and beautiful country we have.

Many of the women you will read about have worked hard to change society, by making people aware of women's rights, by having laws changed or by setting an example. Some were the first or only woman in their field and faced obstacles, isolation and loneliness. But they had the courage to cut new paths for others to follow. These great Canadian women can be an inspiration to all Canadians to follow their dreams.

> "WE WANT WOMEN LEADERS TODAY AS NEVER BEFORE ... I THINK WOMEN CAN SAVE CIVILIZATION."
>
> — Emily Murphy

All Born in Canada?

Not all of the great women you'll meet in this book were born in Canada. Some came to Canada to escape discrimination and find a better life. Many accompanied their parents or husbands and fell in love with the land. Others were here for only a short while, but during that time they made a lasting impression. These women are included in this book because they've helped make Canada great.

"MANY CANADIAN WOMEN WORK TIRELESSLY TO IMPROVE THEIR LIVES AND THE LIVES OF OTHERS, BOTH IN CANADA AND AROUND THE WORLD. SOME OF THESE WOMEN RECEIVE LITTLE RECOGNITION FOR THEIR EFFORTS, YET PROVIDE SHINING EXAMPLES FOR CANADIANS AND CANADIAN YOUTH IN PARTICULAR TO FOLLOW THEIR DREAMS, NO MATTER WHAT BARRIERS AND OPPOSITION THEY MAY FACE."

— *Jean Augustine*

Changing Place Names

Some of the provinces and territories have changed their names during the lives of the great Canadians. In this book, the current provincial or territorial name is usually used. Here are some of the older names:

- Ontario was known as Upper Canada from 1791 to 1840 and then as Canada West from 1841 to 1867.
- Quebec was New France from 1608 to 1763, the Province of Quebec from 1763 to 1791, Lower Canada from 1791 to 1840 and Canada East from 1841 to 1867.

- Alberta and Saskatchewan were part of the Northwest Territories until 1905.
- Nunavut was part of the Northwest Territories before 1999.
- Newfoundland changed its name to Newfoundland and Labrador in 2001.

HEROES

Brave, determined, bold, unselfish — the great Canadian women you'll meet here had these characteristics and more. Some of them had the courage to risk their lives to help others. Others were determined to change things for the better.

You'll read about women from all walks of life, some who lived more than 300 years ago and others who are alive today. Whatever their backgrounds and whenever they lived, their heroism continues to inspire us.

The Famous Five

> **Reformers**
>
> **Formed:** 1927, at Edmonton, AB
>
> **Disbanded:** October 18, 1929, at Edmonton, AB

Henrietta Muir Edwards, Nellie McClung; Louise McKinney, Emily Murphy and Irene Parlby were women who worked hard to improve women's lives. They fought to get women the right to vote, battled for a minimum wage for women, struggled to improve farm women's rights and more.

By 1917 Canadian women were pushing the prime minister to make Emily Murphy a senator. Some people opposed women being appointed to the Senate. They argued that when the British North America (BNA) Act talked of "persons" being appointed to the Senate, it meant men, so a woman couldn't become a senator.

Emily wouldn't accept this. When she discovered that a group of five could challenge such a ruling, she gathered four friends and they sent a petition to the Supreme Court of Canada. But the Court said no — the term "persons" in the BNA Act did not include women.

The "Famous Five" didn't give up. The Persons Case, as it came to be called, was appealed to the judges of the Privy Council of England, then Canada's highest authority. On October 18, 1929, the English judges said that the word "persons" in the BNA Act included men *and* women. Thanks to the Famous Five, women could now hold any government office. Women took another big step towards equality.

> "THE PURPOSE OF A WOMAN'S LIFE IS JUST THE SAME AS THE PURPOSE OF A MAN'S LIFE: THAT SHE MAY MAKE THE BEST POSSIBLE CONTRIBUTION TO HER GENERATION."
>
> — *Louise McKinney*

Henrietta Muir Edwards (1849–1931) helped found the National Council of Women of Canada.

Nellie McClung (1873–1951) headed the fight to get Canadian women the vote.

Louise McKinney (1868–1931) was the first woman elected to a provincial legislature.

Emily Murphy (1868–1933) became the first woman magistrate in Canada.

Irene Parlby (1868–1965) was the first female member of the Cabinet (advisors to the premier) in Alberta.

Louise Arbour

Judge and human rights advocate

Born: *Feb. 10, 1947, at Montreal, PQ*

Louise Arbour is known internationally as a fighter for human rights. On July 1, 2004, she became the United Nations High Commissioner for Human Rights, the first Canadian to have this responsibility. Her role is to give a voice to victims around the world whose rights have been abused.

It required courage for Louise to accept this position — the man she replaced was killed by a bomb. She took the job despite the danger and has earned the respect of many human rights groups.

Before taking on the Commissioner's job, Louise had sought justice for the victims of war crimes at the International Criminal Tribunal for Rwanda and the former Yugoslavia. Then she was appointed to the Supreme Court of Canada, only the fourth woman to achieve this important position (find out about other women Supreme Court judges on pages 49, 58 and 60).

Smart and determined, Louise feels that terrorism is the biggest challenge facing people fighting for human rights anywhere. Canadians are proud of the important role she has played in protecting those rights around the world.

Laura Secord

Hero of the War of 1812

Born: *Sept. 13, 1775, at Great Barrington, MA, U.S.*

Died: *Oct. 17, 1868, at Chippawa (now Niagara Falls), ON*

The War of 1812 was a bitter two-year battle between the United States and Britain for control of Canada. When American officers forced their way into Laura Secord's house in Queenston, Ontario, on June 21, 1813, she had to agree to their demands for rooms and food.

While the officers dined, Laura overheard their plans for a surprise attack on the British soldiers at Beaver Dams, about 32 km (20 mi.) away. *Someone has to warn the British,* thought Laura. Her husband was

LAURA SECORD *LEGENDARY PATRIOT*
HÉROÏNE LÉGENDAIRE

CANADA 42

wounded and too weak to go. It was up to her.

The land was wild and the walking difficult, but Laura struggled on. She couldn't take main roads

DID YOU KNOW

You can visit the home where Laura Secord's famous walk began. Laura Secord Homestead, in Queenston near Niagara Falls, has been restored to look the way it did when Laura lived there.

because American soldiers might stop her — and even shoot her. Despite swamps, forests and blazing sun, Laura got her message to the British defenders.

Two days later the U.S. attackers were ambushed and had to surrender. Laura had saved the Niagara area from being taken over by the Americans.

Jeanne Mance

Nurse

Born: *about Nov. 12, 1606, at Langres, France*

Died: *June 18, 1673, at Montreal, PQ*

Growing up in a wealthy family in France, Jeanne Mance could have lived a life of luxury. Instead, she decided to become a nurse and travel to a new colony on the other side of the ocean.

In 1641, Jeanne sailed for New France (today's Quebec). A year later she travelled to Ville-Marie (now Montreal) and began working with the sick and injured there. She founded a hospital, the Hôtel-Dieu de Montréal, which was completed in 1645. Although it had just eight beds, it was an important addition to the tiny colony.

Life was hard in Ville-Marie. Treating battle wounds, sickness and disease kept Jeanne very busy. She cared for the sick throughout her life with enthusiasm and energy. She even sailed back to France several times to get help for the colony.

Today, one of Health Canada's buildings in Ottawa is named in Jeanne's honour. In Montreal you can visit a museum dedicated to her, as well as Parc Jeanne-Mance.

Harriet Tubman

Underground Railroad conductor

Born: *about 1820, in Dorchester County, MD, U.S.*

Died: *Mar. 10, 1913, at Auburn, NY, U.S.*

Harriet Tubman hated being a slave. She'd heard of the Underground Railroad, a secret network of people who helped slaves escape from southern American states, where slavery was legal, to the northern states and Canada. The Railroad helped Harriet escape, and she decided to free other slaves.

A woman couldn't be a "conductor" on the Railroad, Harriet was told. But she refused to accept this and went to the American South 19 times to bring back slaves. There was no turning back once on their way. Harriet would pull out her gun and say, "Dead men tell no tales. Go on or die." None of her "passengers" was ever caught.

Although there was a $40 000 reward for Harriet's capture, she was never caught either. This was especially amazing since she suffered from narcolepsy, a disease that makes people suddenly fall asleep.

Harriet lived in Canada from 1851 to 1861 and helped many Black people settle in the St. Catharines area. She was the Underground Railroad's most successful conductor and freed about 300 slaves. By 1861, when she returned to live in the United States, Harriet had helped many new Canadian families make their start.

"THERE'S TWO THINGS I'VE GOT A RIGHT TO, AND THESE ARE DEATH OR LIBERTY — ONE OR THE OTHER I MEAN TO HAVE."

— *Harriet Tubman*

Armine Gosling

Suffragist

Born: 1861, at Waterloo, PQ

Died: Dec. 5, 1942, in Bermuda

Extreme poverty was all Armine Nutting knew while she was growing up in a small town near Montreal. Her mother insisted that education was the best way to escape this life and made sure that Armine and her brothers and sister went to school.

Armine studied hard and was eventually hired as principal at a girls' school in St. John's, Newfoundland, in 1882. She was soon desperately homesick but

didn't have enough money to return home. Armine would live in Newfoundland for most of her life.

In 1888 Armine married Gilbert Gosling, who became quite wealthy. What a change for Armine! But she never forgot how hard her mother had worked and was anxious to help poor children and women. She knew that conditions for women would change only if they could vote and change the laws. Women who fought for the right to vote, or suffrage, were called suffragists.

A spellbinding speaker and writer, Armine was a founder of the suffragist movement in Newfoundland. In 1925

women finally won the right to vote in Newfoundland, thanks to Armine and her pride in women and their work.

Madeleine de Verchères

Hero of New France

Born: Mar. 3, 1678, at Verchères, PQ

Died: Aug. 8, 1747, at Sainte-Anne-de-la-Perade, PQ

This hero's real name was Marie-Madeleine Jarret, but she's become famous as Madeleine de Verchères because she saved her family's home, Fort Verchères.

When Madeleine was growing up in New France (now Quebec), there were constant battles between the Huron and Iroquois peoples for control of the fur trade. As allies of the Hurons, the French were involved in these fights. But by fall 1692, all seemed peaceful. So Madeleine's parents travelled from their fort on business, leaving just an old soldier in charge.

DID YOU KNOW

When Madeleine de Verchères was 12, her mother, Marie, held off a two-day Iroquois attack. Madeleine helped — and learned a lot about courage.

Without warning on October 22, 1692, the Iroquois attacked. Madeleine, just 14, was working outside the fort and barely made it to safety inside the gate. She took command of the fort, yelling and waving her arms so the Iroquois would think lots of soldiers were inside. She knew how to use a musket and was a good shot.

Madeleine fired off a cannon to signal nearby forts to send help from Montreal. Then she spent a sleepless night watching the fort's walls for attackers.

The next day the Iroquois gave up — just before help arrived. Madeleine had saved the fort.

Georgina Pope

Military nurse

Born: *Jan. 1, 1862, at Charlottetown, PE*

Died: *June 6, 1938, at Charlottetown, PE*

A pampered, well-off life was what most people thought was ahead for Cecily Jane Georgina Fane Pope. After all, her father was wealthy and a Father of Confederation, one of the men who had united Canada in 1867.

But Georgina's family lost its money, so she decided to become a nurse. In those days, nursing wasn't seen as a respectable job, but Georgina was determined. Her organization skills made her an excellent nurse and manager.

When the South African (Boer) War broke out in 1899, Georgina signed up. She was one of the first Canadian military nurses to serve overseas. Georgina had to deal with horrible wounds, scorpions, fever epidemics and much more. In 1903 she was awarded the Royal Red Cross medal, becoming the first Canadian to win this honour.

Soon Georgina became head of the Nursing Service for Canada's Army Medical Corps. When World War I broke out in Europe in 1914, she continued training nurses. In 1917 she was sent to France.

Georgina later collapsed from stress. Her work was over, but her heroism had saved many lives and changed how people think of nurses.

Mary Dohey

Flight attendant

Born: *Sept. 22, 1933, at St. Bride's, NF*

The Cross of Valour is Canada's highest award for bravery. It's only awarded to Canadians who show extreme courage. Mary Dohey was the first living person to win this great honour.

On November 12, 1971, Mary, a flight attendant, was on a flight between Calgary and Toronto. Not long after takeoff, a man took over the plane and held a shotgun to her head.

Mary tried to remain calm and talk gently with the hijacker, even though he threatened to shoot her. When the plane landed at the hijacker's chosen destination of Great Falls, Montana, Mary convinced him to let all the passengers go. Then the hijacker said the rest of the crew had to stay—but she could go.

Mary knew that she had influence over the hijacker, so she stayed on board when the plane took off again. As the hijacker prepared to parachute out of the plane, he put down his gun for an instant. The captain jumped him and hurled the gun away. The eight-hour ordeal was over. Mary was a hero.

DID YOU KNOW

Two other women have won the Cross of Valour. Anna Lang rescued friends from a car accident, and Jean Swedberg died helping others escape from a hotel fire.

Viola Desmond

Black rights activist

Born: *July 6, 1914, at Halifax, NS*

Died: *1965*

When Viola Desmond's car broke down in New Glasgow, Nova Scotia, on November 9, 1946, she didn't know she was about to make history. Stuck in New Glasgow overnight, this quiet hairdresser bought a movie ticket and sat in the theatre's main floor section. She didn't notice her ticket was for the balcony. Only White people could sit on the main floor. Black people had to sit upstairs.

When told to move, Viola tried to buy a ticket for the main floor. The teller refused. This was the last straw. Viola had put up with enough racial discrimination. She returned to the main floor and sat until a policeman carried her out.

The next day Viola was charged with cheating the Province of Nova Scotia. The balcony-seat ticket that she'd bought was cheaper by one cent of tax than the main-floor seat she'd sat in. Mention of skin colour was carefully avoided. Viola was found guilty.

Viola fought her conviction, and many people, including newspaper publisher Carrie Best (page 58), helped. Although she lost all of her appeals, Viola had the courage to battle discrimination. Finally, in 1954, Nova Scotia outlawed racial segregation (separation due to race).

Marie de La Tour

Acadian hero

Born: *1602, in France*

Died: *about May 8, 1645, at Fort La Tour, NB*

Françoise-Marie Jacquelin was an adventurous woman. In 1640 she agreed to marry a man she'd never met, Charles de Saint-Étienne de La Tour, and leave France to live in a place she'd never been, Acadia.

Acadia was the name for part of today's Nova Scotia, New Brunswick and Prince Edward Island. At the time, it was a colony of France. The French king put Marie's husband and Charles de Menou d'Aulnay in charge of Acadia. The two men fought, killing soldiers and blockading each other's forts.

In April 1645, d'Aulnay learned that Marie's husband was away. Before de La Tour could return, d'Aulnay attacked. Marie commanded her 45 soldiers bravely, but the enemy had two ships full of men. At first she refused to surrender. Then d'Aulnay promised to spare the lives of everyone in the fort, and Marie gave in.

Poor Marie had to watch as d'Aulnay went back on his word and hanged her soldiers. She died three weeks later in prison, but her courageous attempt to resist the attack has never been forgotten.

Marie de La Tour's home in Acadia was a rough log building, but inside were fine pottery and glass and expensive, beautiful furnishings.

INNOVATORS

An innovator is someone who begins or introduces something new. Canadian women innovators have made their mark in human rights, journalism, sports and many other fields. They saw new ways of doing things and took risks to make them happen.

It takes courage for a woman to be different, to look at problems or situations and come up with new solutions. Then it usually takes very hard work to make those changes. These clever and innovative women show that, with enough determination, any change is possible.

Mary Ann Shadd

Black rights activist

Born: *Oct. 9, 1823, at Wilmington, DE, U.S.*

Died: *June 5, 1893, at Washington, DC, U.S.*

The importance of education was something Mary Ann Shadd learned as a child. She was born in the state of Delaware, where it was against the law to educate Black people. When she was just 10, she was sent to school in Pennsylvania.

In 1851, the United States passed a law allowing Black people to be sold into slavery, even if they'd never been enslaved. At age 28 Mary Ann fled to Windsor, Ontario. There, she found that Black and White people lived in separate communities. Mary Ann did not agree with this — she felt Black and White people should live together. She set up a school for Black children who had escaped to Canada on the Underground Railroad (find out more about it on page 8) and encouraged White children to attend as well.

When White parents refused to send their children to Mary Ann's school, she decided that parents also needed to be educated. So she started the *Provincial Freeman* newspaper, becoming the first Black woman in North America to run a newspaper. Mary Ann published articles against racial segregation and slavery and exposed discrimination. She also

"YOU HAVE A RIGHT TO YOUR FREEDOM AND TO EVERY OTHER PRIVILEGE CONNECTED WITH IT …"

— *Mary Ann Shadd*

wrote about women's contributions to society and their rights.

Mary Ann was criticized by both Blacks and Whites for her opinions, but she kept publishing. She was ahead of her time and felt sure that the future would be better for everyone if the races learned to live together in harmony.

Elizabeth Arden

Businesswoman

Born: Dec. 31, 1878, at Woodbridge, ON

Died: Oct. 19, 1966, at New York City, NY, U.S.

Before Elizabeth Arden began her cosmetics business, most women didn't wear makeup. Elizabeth changed that. She took makeup from the theatre stage and made it available to all women.

Elizabeth's real name was Florence Nightingale Graham, after the famous nurse. Florence tried nursing but found she was too squeamish. Creating beauty creams suited her much better.

Although Florence's family thought she should marry and drop the idea of her own cosmetics business, she never gave up on her dream. Instead, she moved to New York, renamed herself Elizabeth Arden and opened a beauty salon. Her drive and business smarts made it an immediate success.

Spotting trends was Elizabeth's best skill. She was constantly making new products and coming up with innovative ideas. She offered the first "makeovers" in her salon and was one of the first to make exercise recordings and give yoga lessons. A pioneer in the world of business, Elizabeth eventually became a multi-millionaire.

Viola MacMillan

Miner and prospector

Born: Apr. 21, 1903, at Windermere, ON

Died: Aug. 26, 1993, Toronto, ON

Viola first got interested in mining when her brother, a silver miner in Cobalt, Ontario, took her underground. She had to go disguised as a man because women were considered unlucky in mines. After spending summers as a part-time prospector, Viola decided in 1930 to make mining her career. She loved the ruggedness of the work.

With her husband, Viola prospected and set up mines across Canada. She had an amazing skill for finding large mineral deposits and

became one of the country's wealthiest business people.

But miners most remember Viola for her organizing work. She took a group of fewer than 100 prospectors and turned it into the Prospectors and Developers Association, with more than 4000 members across the country. Thanks to Viola, who was president for almost 30 years, the group has become known around the world.

Viola spent time in jail in the 1960s because of a mining scandal. But she was fully pardoned a few years later and was recognized for her contributions to mining. In 1993 she became a member of the Canadian Mining Hall of Fame.

"I ALWAYS BELIEVED THAT WOMEN COULD DO ANYTHING MEN COULD, IF THEY WERE JUST PREPARED TO PUT THEIR MINDS TO IT AND GET DOWN TO WORK."

— Viola MacMillan

Deanna Brasseur

Canada's first woman jet fighter pilot

Born: Sept. 9, 1953, at Pembroke, ON

When Deanna Brasseur joined the Canadian Armed Forces in 1972, women in the military were mostly secretaries, nurses and food staff. Dee was a typist, and her uniform included a purse, gloves, blouse and skirt — not pants.

In 1979 the military began a trial program to train women as pilots. Dee signed up immediately. Some of the men in her training group pretended she didn't exist. Others told her she shouldn't be there.

But Dee loved flying. She became Canada's first female flight instructor and first female flight commander. On February 17, 1989, Captains Deanna Brasseur and Jane Foster became the first female fighter pilots in Canada. The $35 million jet Dee flew was the most powerful in the Canadian Air Force.

Two years later Dee — now a major — became Canada's first female aircraft accident investigator, monitoring the activities of all Canadian military jet trainer and fighter aircraft. Dee has never forgotten how badly she was treated during training and is very supportive of other women in the Air Force.

"I WASN'T THERE TO CONVINCE THE GUYS THAT WOMEN SHOULD BE PILOTS. I WAS THERE BECAUSE I WANTED TO BE A PILOT."

— *Deanna Brasseur*

Doris Anderson

Editor and activist

Born: Nov. 10, 1925, at Calgary, AB

As a teenager, Hilda Doris Buck found it difficult to accept her mother's view of a traditional life with marriage and children. Instead, Doris put herself through university and decided to be a journalist. But there were few journalism jobs open to women. So she worked in advertising at *Chatelaine*, a women's magazine that, like most, featured recipes and beauty tips.

Doris worked her way up and, in 1956, became *Chatelaine's* editor. Wanting to give readers "something serious to think about, something to shake them up," she included articles on human rights, equal pay and tips for working women. Some readers didn't like the changes, but

many women appreciated what Doris was doing. Sales soared.

That same year, Doris married David Anderson. As Doris Anderson she became famous across Canada for fighting for women's rights. She edited *Chatelaine* until 1977, then became head of the Canadian Advisory Council on the Status of Women. From 1982 to 1984 Doris was president of the National Action Committee on the Status of Women. Her work on these committees and her journalism have changed the way Canadian women see themselves and their country.

Maureen Kempston-Darkes

Businesswoman

Born: Jul. 31, 1948, at Toronto, ON

It's a long way from working as a receptionist at a car dealership to being the president of General Motors (GM) of Canada. But that's the road that Maureen Kempston-Darkes has driven along. From 1994 to 2001 she was the first woman president of GM of Canada.

Today, more and more Canadian women are working in top positions for car manufacturers. For instance, Cynthia Trudell was the chairman and president of Saturn Corporation, while Bobbi Gaunt was the president of the Ford Motor Company of Canada Ltd. "I'm pleased that the old stereotype of the auto industry being a male preserve no longer applies," says Maureen.

Maureen feels that girls need to be educated in science and technology. She also suggests that volunteering is a great way to develop skills. And Maureen stresses the importance of girls and women supporting each other. She believes it's vital to share experiences and contribute to the development of others.

Kate Aitken

Broadcaster and writer

Born: Apr. 6, 1891, at Beeton, ON

Died: Dec. 11, 1971, at Streetsville, ON

Talk about a lucky break — Kate Aitken got her start in radio in 1934 when another commentator had an accident and broke a hip. Kate filled in — then stayed on the air for the next 24 years. When she broadcast in the 1940s and 1950s, she had 3 million listeners, or about one-quarter of all Canadians!

A food-preserving business was the start of Kate's career in the 1910s. She moved on to become one of the first women lecturers for the Ontario Department of Agriculture, and later a consultant to a chain of drug stores, a cooking teacher and the women's editor of the *Montreal Standard* newspaper. "Mrs. A." was also heard on the radio twice a week across the country.

Kate believed women should be independent and that they could balance career and home. Life was an adventure to her, and she encouraged people to try new things. If they failed, she told them to try again. Kate's positive attitude in her writing and radio shows inspired Canadian women, especially during World War II.

DID YOU KNOW

Kate Aitken interviewed many famous people, including Canada's prime ministers, Queen Elizabeth, Franklin D. Roosevelt and even Adolf Hitler.

Adelaide Hoodless

Reformer

Born: Feb. 26, 1857, at St. George, ON

Died: Feb. 26, 1910, at Toronto, ON

Some women become innovators because of a single event. In 1889 Adelaide Hoodless unknowingly gave her son contaminated milk, and he died. Adelaide was heartbroken — and furious that she hadn't known better. She was determined that no other women would suffer such anguish.

Adelaide dedicated the rest of her life to educating women, especially about homemaking and cleanliness. She helped Lady Aberdeen (below) found the

National Council of Women of Canada and the Victorian Order of Nurses. She also helped create the national YWCA of Canada.

But Adelaide is most remembered for founding the Women's Institute in 1897. This practical, self-help organization developed the skills and confidence of rural women. It was a success from the start, and some people think it is Canada's greatest export. Today more than 8 million women around the world belong to the Women's Institute, and Adelaide's vision continues to inspire them.

"EDUCATE A BOY AND YOU EDUCATE A MAN, BUT EDUCATE A GIRL AND YOU EDUCATE A FAMILY."

— *Adelaide Hoodless*

Ishbel Gordon, Lady Aberdeen

Reformer

Born: Mar. 15, 1857, at London, England

Died: Apr. 18, 1939, at Aberdeen, Scotland

Although Lady Aberdeen only lived in Canada from 1893 to 1898, while her husband was Governor General, she made many changes that helped Canadian women.

Ishbel Maria Gordon, Countess of Aberdeen, was a wealthy, powerful woman with a strong social conscience. She travelled with her husband across Canada, talking to women from many backgrounds. Canadian women were a huge unused resource, she decided, and

they could contribute a great deal to Canada's development. Important people laughed at her ideas, but she didn't let that stop her.

Lady Aberdeen helped set up the National Council of Women of Canada in 1893 and became the first president of the International Council of Women. She also formed the Victorian Order of Nurses, an organization that cares for sick people in their own homes.

In 1897 Lady Aberdeen received an honorary degree from Queen's University in Kingston, Ontario. That made her the first woman given this tribute by a Canadian university. She was appreciated by ordinary Canadians because she tried to break down the class barriers between the wealthy and the poor.

Peg Seller

Inventor of synchronized swimming

Born: *Jan. 23, 1905, at Edinburgh, Scotland*

Died: *Mar. 31, 1996, at Newmarket, ON*

Did you know the first swimmers to perform dances in water weren't women? They were men! But they didn't use music and there were no rules. That changed in the 1920s when Margaret Shearer (later Seller) and two friends began developing a sport for swimmers who weren't interested in speed swimming.

With her friends, Peg created what they called "ornamental and scientific swimming," or "fancy swimming," using swimming and life-saving techniques and performing them to music. Peg set rules and organized the first competition in 1924. An excellent swimmer, she won first prize.

Peg was a pioneer in the sport and continued to develop it. In 1938 she set standards for judging at competitions. The sport was now called synchronized swimming, and as its popularity spread, Peg wrote the rules for international competition.

Synchronized swimming is one of the few sports developed *by* women *for* women. In 1984 it became an official Olympic event, and Canadians began scooping up medals. Carolyn Waldo and Sylvie Frechette are probably the country's most famous synchro swimmers because of the Olympic gold medals they've won.

Elsie MacGill

Engineer

Born: *Mar. 27, 1905, at Vancouver, BC*

Died: *Nov. 4, 1980, at Cambridge, MA, U.S.*

When Elizabeth MacGill decided to become an engineer, no one in her family discouraged her from entering this traditionally male field. After all, both her mother and grandmother were suffragists (women who fought for the vote for women), and her mother was the first female judge in British Columbia.

In 1927 Elsie graduated from the University of Toronto, the first woman graduate in electrical engineering in Canada. But in 1929

she came down with polio (a disease that can cause paralysis). Elsie was told she would never walk again. Undaunted, she eventually taught herself to walk using canes.

Elsie had many "firsts" in her life. She designed the Maple Leaf II Trainer, a plane used to test pilots, making her the world's first female aircraft designer. Her disability prevented her from being a pilot, but she made sure she was a passenger on all of the plane's test flights.

During World War II (1939–1945), Elsie was head of airplane production for Canada. After the war she continued in engineering but also campaigned for daycare, paid maternity leave and other changes to make women's lives better.

"I'M AN ENGINEER AND I DO WHAT ALL ENGINEERS DO, THAT'S ALL."

— *Elsie MacGill*

PERFORMERS

Canadian women bring a unique flavour to music, television, stage and film. They present our country to the world and, because of them, many people in other countries first become interested in Canada.

You may be surprised to find out that a Canadian woman was Hollywood's first megastar or that women from Canada have set international records for music sales. These great Canadian women have changed the world of entertainment.

Karen Kain

Dancer

Born: Mar. 28, 1951, at Hamilton, ON

At age eight Karen Kain wrote, "When I grow up I am going to be a ballerina … It will be so much fun being a ballerina." Karen was inspired to become a ballerina after watching dancer Celia Franca, who was also founder and director of the National Ballet of Canada.

It was tough for Karen to leave her home in Hamilton at age 11 to attend the National Ballet School in Toronto. Betty Oliphant, founding director of the school, encouraged Karen and her parents. When the Kains found it difficult to afford Karen's fees, Betty assured them that Karen was very talented and their money was well spent. Karen was just 18 when she joined the National Ballet Company in 1969.

Karen wasn't a natural ballerina. Her back was too long and her hips weren't flexible enough. But she wouldn't accept these limitations, even when the hours of daily practice caused her intense pain. She quickly became a principal dancer and soloist.

With her excellent technique, range of movement and skill at interpreting music, Karen was a star in both classical and contemporary ballets. She retired from dancing in 1997 and later became the artistic director of the National Ballet of Canada.

Other ballerinas who have won the hearts of Canadian audiences include Veronica Tennant, who also wrote two ballet books for kids, and Evelyn Hart, a very graceful and dramatic dancer.

DID YOU KNOW

Karen Kain first took dance classes because her mother wanted her to improve her posture.

Céline Dion

Céline Dion was just five years old when she began singing on weekends at her parents' restaurant. She quickly learned how to captivate an audience, one of the skills that has helped turn her into an international superstar.

All of Céline's family were musical, but her mother realized that the youngest of her 14 children had something special. At age 13, Céline released a hit single and, in just a few years, was Quebec's most popular female singer. She was soon recording in both English and French and making smash hits. Some of her most popular songs are from movies, including *Beauty and the Beast* and *Titanic*.

An incredible voice, strict discipline and strong determination have put Céline at the top. Over her career she has sold more than 130 million albums. She was the first Canadian to earn a gold record in France and continues to win international awards. But Céline takes time to increase awareness about cystic fibrosis, a disease that killed one of her nieces.

Mary Pickford

Making films was not something teenage stage actor Gladys Louise Smith wanted to do. She felt movies were second rate. But she was tired of being poor. When she got a chance to audition for a movie in New York, with much better pay, she changed her mind. She also changed her name — to Mary Pickford — and went on to become a movie star, then a superstar. In the 1910s and 1920s, Mary was the most famous woman alive.

Mary was able to quickly adjust her acting style to suit the movies, and audiences loved the spunky characters she played. She soon became known as America's Sweetheart.

At a time when most women didn't have jobs or careers, Mary earned as much as $350 000 per movie, a huge amount then. By age 24, she was Hollywood's first millionaire ever.

When movie studios could no longer afford Mary's salary, she joined with other movie superstars to start their own studio, United Artists Pictures. Mary won two Academy Awards, but, more important, she changed how people thought about independent women.

"THE PAST CANNOT BE CHANGED. THE FUTURE IS YET IN YOUR POWER."

— *Mary Pickford*

Shania Twain

Singer

Born: *Aug. 28, 1965, at Windsor, ON*

Eileen Edwards sang all the time, even when walking down the street, much to the embarrassment of her siblings. She didn't have much to sing about — her family was poor and often couldn't afford heat or enough to eat.

It was Eileen's mother and stepfather who introduced her to country music. Sadly, they were both killed in a car accident when Eileen was 21. All of a sudden it was up to her to support her family.

Eileen continued to sing, now at clubs and in shows. She changed her name to Shania Twain (Shania is an Ojibwa name that means "I'm on my way," and Twain was her Ojibwa stepfather's last name) and recorded her first album.

Her next recording won Shania a 1996 Grammy Award, one of music's highest honours, as Best Country Album. And *Come On Over*, her third album, became the biggest-selling country album of all time, as well as the most successful album by a woman solo artist ever.

Shania's ability to connect with her audiences has made her world famous. She continues to delight fans with her CDs and performances and is also creating a charity to help underprivileged children.

"YOU NEVER KNOW WHAT'S AROUND THE NEXT CORNER, BUT YOU HAVE TO BE WILLING TO EXPLORE IT."

— *Shania Twain*

Sarah Polley

Actor and activist

Born: *Jan. 8, 1979, at Toronto, ON*

A desire to make movies that are important to society is what drives actor and director Sarah Polley. She first appeared in a movie when she was six. Later, she became an international hit as Sara Stanley in the television series *Road to Avonlea*. (It was based on stories by Lucy Maud Montgomery, page 40.)

Sarah's early years were difficult. Her mother died of cancer shortly after Sarah turned 11 — as had

happened to her character, Sara Stanley. Four years later, Sarah also had to go through the pain of surgery to correct scoliosis, a

problem with the curve of the spine.

Being politically active is very important to Sarah. She once lost some teeth after being hit by a policeman during a protest against the Ontario government's policies on poverty. But Sarah always comes back to working in movies. Known for her expressive face, Sarah has an exceptional ability to make viewers understand a character's thoughts. While she looks forward to acting in more films, she also is becoming known as a skilled director.

Kate Reid

Actor

Born: *Nov. 4, 1930, at London, England*

Died: *Mar. 27, 1993, at Stratford, ON*

"I was always tripping on things — breaking bones, knocking myself out, catching pneumonia — and I was out of school a lot." That's how Daphne Kate Reid remembered her childhood. She was born with deformed feet, which were corrected when she was eight. But Kate's feet made her feel different from other kids, like an outsider.

It was Kate's vivid imagination that made her early years bearable.

"The idea of being someone else rather than who I was appealed to me," she once said.

When Kate began studying drama at age 15, her life was changed forever. Critics recognized Kate's talent immediately, and she was a success right from the start. She could play many different types of characters with energy, power and warmth.

Some of the world's best playwrights admired Kate so much that they wrote roles especially for her. This hard-working, disciplined actor was a star in television and movies, as well as on the stage, and won many awards.

"ACTING IS NOT BEING EMOTIONAL, BUT BEING ABLE TO EXPRESS EMOTION."

— *Kate Reid*

Susan Aglukark

Singer and songwriter

Born: *Jan. 27, 1967, at Churchill, MB*

Joy, strength, love of community and hope for the future shine through in Susan Aglukark's music. But she never intended to be a star and at first didn't much like performing alone. She just wanted to sing. Susan sang throughout her childhood, which was spent moving with her family around the Keewatin region of the Northwest Territories (now Nunavut). Eventually, her family settled in Arviat, a small community on Hudson Bay.

Susan's first album was a hit with both country and Aboriginal music fans and, in 1994, won the first Aboriginal Achievement Award in Arts and Entertainment. She continues to record albums and win new fans.

Susan writes from a very personal point of view that shows a strong connection to the Arctic and to her roots. Her message is positive, even though she sings about the often sad history of the Inuit people. That's why she's sometimes called a "pop star with a purpose."

"I've never considered myself a performer-singer," says Susan. "I'm a storyteller-singer more than anything." Through her songs and the awards she has won, Susan has become one of Canada's most famous Aboriginal people.

Emma Albani

Opera singer

Born: *Nov. 1, 1847, at Chambly, PQ*

Died: *Apr. 3, 1930, at London, England*

Marie-Louise-Emma-Cécile Lajeunesse was the first Canadian-born opera singer to become an international star. She began training at age four and sang in public for the first time when she was nine. In the late 1860s, audiences thought opera singers should have Italian names, so she changed her name to Emma Albani.

Composers and conductors loved working with Emma because she had a beautiful, clear voice and had been trained well. She could sing in French, English, Italian and German and learned new operas quickly.

Soon Emma became such a star in Europe that she was called "the queen of song." Fans pulled her carriage through the streets. Once, when she was leaving the island of Malta in the Mediterranean, all the nearby British navy ships formed two lines to salute her. Emma also became a good friend of England's Queen Victoria.

Canada has produced many female opera stars who have followed in Emma's footsteps. In the past, Maureen Forrester, Lois Marshall, Teresa Stratas and Portia White delighted opera fans around the world. Today Isabel Bayrakdarian and Measha Brueggergosman continue to thrill audiences.

When Emma Albani performed, fans often threw flowers or jewellery on stage. Once she was hit in the face by a jewellery case! Luckily, she wasn't seriously injured.

Fiona Reid

Actor

Born: *July 24, 1951, at Kent, England*

The daughter of a British military family, Fiona Reid lived in England, Germany, Africa and the United States before moving to Canada when she was 12 years old. Fiona first became interested in acting in high school, in Toronto. By her early twenties, she was famous across the country as a TV star with a lead role in *King of Kensington*. It was the most successful Canadian TV series of the 1970s.

You can still see Fiona on TV. She has appeared in the shows

Jacob Two-Two and *Road to Avonlea*. However, now she is best known for her roles in films, such as *My Big Fat Greek Wedding*, and on stage.

In theatres across Canada, Fiona has played lead roles. Audiences love her because she gives them the sense that she's truly enjoying herself. Extremely elegant on stage, Fiona can also be very outspoken.

After playing so many roles on television, stage and in the movies, what does Fiona like best about acting? "What I love the most and am most proud of is the absolute joy of living in somebody else's skin."

Diana Krall

Jazz performer

Born: *Nov. 16, 1964, at Nanaimo, BC*

A soothing voice, amazing piano skills and a strong sense of what works best for her have made Diana Krall a jazz superstar. Both her mom and dad played piano, and her whole family used to play music together at least once a week.

Diana began studying classical piano when she was just four. However, she switched to jazz in high school. At 15, she began playing in a local restaurant.

Gradually, Diana shifted from being a jazz pianist who sang occasionally to being one of jazz's top-selling singers. Her third album made her an international star, and her sixth album won a Grammy award for Jazz Vocal Album of the Year in 1999. Four years later so did Diana's album *Live in Paris*. Fans have made her one of jazz's top-selling singers.

Diana continues to evolve as a musician. Instead of just singing well-known jazz songs, she's begun writing her own songs. With her classy and refined style, she has made her mark on jazz music all over the world.

Sarah McLachlan

Singer and songwriter

Born: *Jan. 28, 1968, at Halifax, NS*

Sarah McLachlan describes her young self as "your typical teenage rebel with a skateboard and a bad attitude." Although she began her music career studying classical guitar, piano and voice, she soon changed to pop. Today she's a talented guitarist and keyboard player, as well as a singer and songwriter. She's known for her very personal lyrics, beautiful melodies and high sweet voice.

Helping other women in music is very important to Sarah. From 1997 to 1999 she organized Lilith Fair, an all-female music festival (Diana Krall, above, was one of its stars). In 1997 it was the most successful North American concert tour and sold more than 22 million CDs. During its three years it also raised more than $7 million for various charities.

One of the many charities that Sarah supports is the Sarah McLachlan Music Outreach program, which gives free music classes to inner-city kids in Vancouver. "As a kid," she says, "music saved my life; having that one thing that I knew I was good at made all the difference."

DID YOU KNOW

At one point Sarah McLachlan's fans called themselves The Fumblers in honour of her third album, *Fumbling Towards Ecstasy*, which sold 3 million copies and made her an international star.

ADVENTURERS

They've flown in space, climbed mountains, trekked overland and explored unknown territory. Meet some brave Canadian women who share a great curiosity and sense of adventure about the world.

Being adventurous wasn't always acceptable if you were a woman — in the past it was considered improper. But these adventurous women refused to be stopped. They demanded the same opportunities and responsibilities as men. Their achievements and explorations prove their equal abilities.

Roberta Bondar

First Canadian woman in space

Born: Dec. 4, 1945, at Sault Ste. Marie, ON

Model rocket ships and space platforms cluttered Roberta Bondar's bedroom when she was a kid. "I've always been interested in space travel," she says. Her parents encouraged her, and so did her aunt, who worked for the National Aeronautics and Space Administration (NASA) in the United States.

Roberta trained as a neurologist, a doctor who specializes in the nervous system. In 1983, when the National Research Council of Canada advertised for astronauts, she applied immediately. The competition was tough, and Roberta was delighted to be chosen.

Despite Roberta's lifelong desire to go into space, she turned down her first opportunity. During her training, she was offered a chance to go on board Russia's *Mir* space station and participate in a study on the effects of weightlessness on women. But Roberta felt she was only invited because she was a woman, not because of her skills as a scientist, so she said no.

Roberta finally flew into space in January 1992 on the American space shuttle *Discovery*. She spent eight days on board, conducting experiments and taking photos. "When you see your own country from space," said Roberta, "it is an extraordinary experience."

Julie Payette was the second Canadian woman in space and, in 1999, became the first Canadian to board the International Space Station. She trained as an engineer and worked on space robotics. Both Julie and Roberta inspire Canadian girls and women to believe "the sky's the limit!"

DID YOU KNOW

Roberta Bondar was one of six Canadians selected from more than 4300 applicants, and Julie Payette was one of four chosen from more than 5300.

Faith Fenton

Journalist

Born: Jan. 14, 1857, at Bowmanville, ON

Died: Jan. 10, 1936, at Toronto, ON

By day, Alice Freeman was a teacher in Toronto. But at night she became Faith Fenton, a reporter writing on everything from women's shelters — and the bedbugs that crawled over her there — to lavish parties held by the most important people in Canada.

During the late 1800s, teachers were expected to be extremely prim. Journalism was considered improper, so Alice concealed her other life by using another name. Women — and men — across Canada loved to read Faith's thoughts on women's lives, politicians and more. She travelled alone across Canada and the United States and got to know many famous women, including Lady Aberdeen (page 16), Emma Albani (page 22) and Emily Stowe (page 37).

Faith became most famous in 1898, when she joined 200 soldiers and four nurses trekking to Dawson, Yukon Territory, during the Gold Rush. They hiked through swampy muskeg and clouds of mosquitoes. Faith sent stories back to the *Globe* newspaper describing the incredibly tough journey and, later, her life in Dawson. She cheered and inspired her readers and encouraged them to make the most of their lives.

Phyllis Munday

Mountaineer

Born: Sept. 24, 1894, in Ceylon (now Sri Lanka)

Died: Apr. 11, 1990, at Vancouver, BC

In the early 1900s, a woman heading out mountain-climbing had to wear a skirt until she was out of public sight. Then she could continue in bloomers, a type of short, baggy pants. That's what Phyllis Munday wore when climbing.

In 1924 Phyl became the first woman to reach the top of Mount Robson, the Rocky Mountains' highest peak. With her husband, Don, she climbed more than 100 mountains. The pair kept careful records of their climbs and snapped many photos.

Phyl also collected insects for a British Columbia museum.

For more than 30 of their ascents, they were the first people to reach the top. But the mountain that fascinated Phyl and Don most was one they never summited, despite 16 attempts. Today it's called Mount Waddington, but the Mundays called it Mystery Mountain.

Phyl encouraged girls and women to try mountaineering. She was also very involved in the Girl Guides and St. John Ambulance. Mount Munday in British Columbia's Coastal Mountains is named after Phyllis and her husband.

"… THERE WAS SOMETHING ABOUT GETTING AWAY OFTEN, IN THE WILDS, AS WE USED TO CALL IT, THAT APPEALED TO ME MORE THAN ANYTHING ELSE, AND I WANTED TO GO UP TO THE MOUNTAINS."

— *Phyllis Munday*

Catherine Schubert

Cross-country traveller

Born: 1835, in Ireland

Died: July 18, 1918, in Armstrong, BC

The Overlanders were a group of about 150 gold seekers who, in 1862, travelled from Ontario across Canada to the Cariboo Mountains in the interior of British Columbia. When Catherine Schubert, her husband and three children joined the group as they passed through Fort Garry (today's Winnipeg) in June 1862, she became the only woman Overlander.

It's difficult to imagine the hardships the Overlanders endured.

Scorching heat, clouds of biting insects and torrential rains were just some of their miseries. There were mountain ledges so narrow that Catherine had to crawl on her hands and knees. And she had a secret that she wouldn't be able to hide for much longer — she was pregnant.

By the time the group began crossing the Rocky Mountains, temperatures were beginning to drop. Snow fell as Catherine's family rafted down the Thompson River. She gave birth to a daughter, Rose, in a small Aboriginal village along the river. A few days later, in mid-October, Catherine and her family finally reached their destination, Fort Kamloops. Their exhausting four-month trek was finally over.

Mina Hubbard

Labrador explorer

Born: 1870, in Bewdley, ON

Died: May 4, 1956, in Coulston, U.K.

Sometimes anger pushes a woman to become an adventurer. When Mina Hubbard's husband died on an unsuccessful expedition across Labrador in 1903, one of the others in the group, Dillon Wallace, wrote a book about their trek. Dillon described Mina's husband, Leonidas, as being weak and unorganized, and that made Mina furious.

So when Dillon announced that he was going to repeat the journey and finish what Leonidas had started, Mina was determined to beat him. She had no experience and was quite a small woman, but she prepared well and hired her husband's guide. The two groups left the Northwest River

Post in June 1905. Mina followed her husband's route along rivers, while Dillon went overland.

Mina's expedition reached Ungava Bay, the final destination, in early September, more than six weeks before Dillon's group. Mina also produced the first accurate map of Labrador's Naskaupi and George Rivers and described in detail the Aboriginal peoples of the area and the great caribou migration.

DID YOU KNOW

Mina Hubbard wrote a book about her journey — *A Woman's Way through Unknown Labrador.* Read it and you'll see that Mina never even mentions Dillon Wallace!

Mary Schäffer Warren

Rocky Mountain explorer

Born: Oct. 4, 1861, at West Chester, PA, U.S.

Died: Jan. 23, 1939, at Banff, AB

As a well-off young girl, Mary Townsend Sharples was interested in art and nature. She also travelled extensively across North America. While in the Rockies in 1889, she met and soon married Dr. Charles Schäffer. Together they studied the area's flowers.

Mary could paint the flowers beautifully, as well as take excellent photos. When Charles died in 1903, Mary continued to record Rocky Mountain flowers, even though it meant venturing into remote areas. At the time, such travel was considered improper for a woman, but Mary didn't care.

After publishing a book of her husband's work with her drawings and photos, Mary began exploring the wilder regions of the Rockies. She became so knowledgeable that, in 1911, the Geological Survey of Canada asked her to map Maligne Lake, near Jasper, Alberta. She also wrote books about the area. In 1915 Mary married Billy Warren, a trail guide, and continued to explore the mountain wilderness she loved and to tell stories about her travels.

"WE CAN STARVE AS WELL AS [MEN] … THE GROUND WILL BE NO HARDER TO SLEEP UPON; THE WATERS NO DEEPER TO SWIM …"

— *Mary Schäffer Warren*

Martha Black

Yukon pioneer and politician

Born: Feb. 24, 1866, at Chicago, IL, U.S.

Died: Nov. 1, 1957, at Whitehorse, YK

Martha Munger Purdy lived a life in Chicago of parties and wealth — and boredom. She wanted adventure. So in 1898 Martha, her husband and her brother headed for Yukon Territory in search of Klondike Gold Rush riches.

The trip was too dangerous, Martha's husband decided, and he quit. But Martha and her brother continued on, climbing the gruelling Chilkoot Trail, a 53 km (33 mi.) path with sections that headed almost straight up. Martha had to wear typical women's clothing: a tight corset, which made breathing difficult, and a heavy long skirt. And she was pregnant. Luckily, she could afford to have someone carry her heavy supplies.

A few months after she reached Dawson City, Martha gave birth, all alone in her cabin. In the years to come, she set up gold mining and sawmill businesses, which were soon successful. Martha eventually remarried, this time to George Black, who became Yukon's Member of Parliament in 1921.

In 1935, George Black was too sick to run for election, so Martha did — and won. That made her only the second woman ever elected to the House of Commons (the first was Agnes Macphail, page 47).

ARTISTS

Thousands of years ago, Native women created pottery, then added decorations to make it unique and beautiful. This was the first art produced in Canada. However, it wasn't until the late 1800s that Canadian women could get a real art education and make art their career.

Today Canadian women paint, draw and sculpt and use everything from quilts and cakes to stone and video to make art. They have been exhibited in the world's best galleries, won major national and international awards and led art organizations across the country.

Emily Carr

Painter

Born: Dec. 13, 1871, at Victoria, BC

Died: Mar. 2, 1945, at Victoria, BC

Today Emily Carr is one of Canada's best-known artists. It's hard to believe that no one really noticed her art until she was 57. Up to then, people didn't understand her bold and unusual paintings.

Emily began drawing when she was eight. In the late 1800s, it was proper for young ladies to paint as a hobby but not as a career. However, Emily was allowed to study art in San Francisco when she was 18 and later in England and France. She developed her distinctive painting style in Paris.

When Emily returned to Victoria in 1912, she decided to visit British Columbia's coastal Aboriginal villages. Many were abandoned, and Emily wanted to sketch them before they disappeared. The Aboriginal culture and west-coast landscapes she saw on her travels inspired her throughout her life.

Emily's paintings were too unusual for the time to sell well. To earn a living — and feed her many pets — she became a landlady, which didn't leave much time for painting.

But after being encouraged by the painters in Canada's famous Group of Seven, Emily returned to her art, painting trees, shores and skies that shimmered with energy.

A heart attack in 1937 forced Emily to cut back on painting, so she turned to writing. Her books were very successful — they're still sold around the world in more than 20 languages. Through her painting and writing, Emily changed the way people see Canada.

DID YOU KNOW

Native people on British Columbia's coast gave Emily Carr the name Klee Wyck (Laughing One). That's what Emily called her first book, and it won the Governor General's Literary Award.

Frances Anne Hopkins

Painter

Born: Feb. 1, 1838, at London, England

Died: Mar. 5, 1919, at London, England

Like Emily Carr (opposite page), Frances Anne Hopkins was expected to draw as a hobby but not make it her career. And she certainly wasn't taught to work with oil paints — they were considered too dirty and smelly for young ladies. People also felt women weren't capable of finishing large oil paintings — female artists were too fragile. But that didn't stop Frances.

Frances came from a family of artists, and her father was an Arctic explorer. So perhaps her family wasn't surprised when she mixed adventure with art by moving to Canada with her husband in 1858 and painting what she saw. Her husband worked for the Hudson's Bay Company and was in charge of fur-trading posts from Montreal to today's Thunder Bay. When he travelled by canoe through this territory, Frances often accompanied him.

The detailed, accurate paintings that Frances created of fur traders at work made her one of Canada's most famous women artists of the 1800s. She was also one of the first artists to paint the upper Great Lakes and western Canada. Frances's works often include images of herself and her husband, as well as white water lilies, her symbol.

Joyce Wieland

Painter, sculptor, printmaker, filmmaker, fabric artist

Born: June 30, 1931, at Toronto, ON

Died: June 27, 1998, at Toronto, ON

Painting, quilting, collage, cartoons, film, knitting — these are just some of the ways that Joyce Wieland expressed her creativity. Her witty, imaginative art challenged the importance of paint and other traditional art materials.

"I WANTED TO ELEVATE AND HONOUR CRAFT, TO JOIN WOMEN TOGETHER AND MAKE THEM PROUD OF WHAT THEY HAD DONE."

— Joyce Wieland

Canada, politics and women's issues all inspired Joyce. To examine the lives of women and women artists, she used craft materials and items found around the home — one of her exhibits included a beautiful cake. Because of this, Joyce had a hard time gaining the respect of many male artists.

Joyce was also an important artist in the world of experimental film in the 1960s. In 1971, she became the first living Canadian woman artist to be the focus of a major exhibition at the National Gallery of Canada. Joyce was one of Canada's most important artists of the second half of the last century and influenced many other artists.

Pitseolak Ashoona and Kenojuak Ashevak

Printmakers and artists

Pitseolak Ashoona

Born: 1904, at Nottingham Island, NT (now NU)

Died: May 28, 1983, at Cape Dorset, NT (now NU)

Kenojuak Ashevak

Born: 1927, at Ikerrasak, NT (now NU)

One of the best-known Inuit artists, Pitseolak Ashoona made prints that are sold around the world. Her work is lively, with a strong sense of balance and design, and often features monsters and spirits.

Pitseolak created more than 7000 drawings and 250 prints, many showing the "old ways" of her people. The success of Pitseolak and other women Inuit artists made them as respected in their communities as the most successful male hunters.

Like Pitseolak, Kenojuak Ashevak has lived in both traditional Inuit and modern North American cultures. Kenojuak grew up sewing beautiful designs on sealskin. In the late 1950s, she was given her first piece of paper to draw on. "A piece of paper from the outside world," she said, "is as thin as the shell of a snowbird's egg." Kenojuak's print *The Enchanted Owl* is one of the most famous works of Inuit art.

Pitseolak Ashoona

Kenojuak Ashevak

Helen McNicoll

Painter

Born: 1879, at Toronto, ON

Died: June 27, 1915, at Swanage, England

One of the first professionally trained Canadian women painters, Helen McNicoll created beautiful paintings of women and their daily work. Children and nature also inspired her. Using small brush strokes, she painted light that made her art glow.

Helen liked to paint outdoors, but it wasn't considered respectable for a woman to be out alone in the late 1800s. So she painted with a friend. A crowd often gathered to see the strange sight of women painting.

Helen was deaf, so her friend also helped her communicate with others.

Not only did Helen win many awards, she also made people aware of the importance of women's work. Other important Canadian women painters of the late 1800s and early 1900s include Florence Carlyle, Laura Muntz Lyall, Mary Hiester Reid, Mary Wrinch Reid and Sidney Strickland Tully. Like Helen McNicoll, they're known for their brushwork and use of light and colour.

Maud Lewis

Painter

Born: Mar. 7, 1903, at South Ohio, NS

Died: July 30, 1970, at Digby, NS

Colourful scenes of rural life in Nova Scotia were what Maud Lewis most liked to paint. Although birth defects left her permanently hunched, and arthritis twisted her fingers, Maud created joyful, bright paintings. The cheerfulness of Maud's art expressed her charming smile and sweet, shy personality.

Maud's paintings looked simple, but each was carefully thought out and skillfully composed. She never had much money so she usually worked with scrounged house paint or boat paint on boards, cardboard and even wallpaper.

Perched on a chair at the front window — it provided the only light in the house — Maud created blue-

eared cats, oxen with long eyelashes and long-beaked birds. Her happy colours brightened people's lives and won her fans across North America.

Maud Lewis and her husband lived in a tiny house — it would fit in most living rooms. Maud painted bright flowers, birds and butterflies on everything, even the stove and windows. You can see the house in the Art Gallery of Nova Scotia in Halifax.

Joanne Tod

Painter

Born: Feb. 12, 1953, at Montreal, PQ

One of Canada's most important artists working today, Joanne Tod is a skilled portrait painter, known for paintings that are almost as realistic as photographs. She often begins with images from ads, magazine illustrations or other popular media and gives them a clever, witty twist.

Using her paintings to comment on modern society, Joanne looks at big subjects such as culture, racism and women's issues. She wants to make people think about these topics and to understand that there are many ways of looking at them. Clever titles help Joanne make her point, and she sometimes even includes words and sentences in her paintings.

Rich fabrics and draperies especially fascinate Joanne. She paints them with intense colours that seem to glow. Joanne deliberately makes the lighting in her works look artificial and unreal so that people will stop and think.

Elizabeth Simcoe

Painter

Born: *around Sept. 22, 1762, in Northamptonshire, England, or Nov. 1766, at Whitchurch, England*

Died: *Jan. 17, 1850, at Devon, England*

Like all wealthy young ladies in England in the 1700s, Elizabeth Posthuma Gwillim was taught foreign languages, music, botany — and watercolour painting. So when she married John Graves Simcoe and travelled with him to Canada in 1791, the diaries she sent home

included beautiful, detailed sketches. John was Upper Canada's first Lieutenant-Governor, which in those days meant he ran the colony.

Elizabeth was enthusiastic and curious, and her journals and careful drawings record what life was like for a well-off lady during pioneer times.

The wild beauty of what is now Ontario inspired Elizabeth, and she enjoyed such adventures as eating raccoon and squirrel, visiting Niagara Falls (she painted it often) and travelling by canoe. Her ability to make accurate drawings was very important, since there were no cameras. The diaries and sketches Elizabeth created provide some of the first information we have about day-to-day life in early Ontario.

Frances Loring
and Florence Wyle

Sculptors

Frances Loring

Born: *Oct. 14, 1887, at Wardner, ID, U.S.*

Died: *Feb. 5, 1968, at Newmarket, ON*

Florence Wyle

Born: *Nov. 24, 1881, at Trenton, IL, U.S.*

Died: *Jan. 14, 1968, at Newmarket, ON*

Frances Loring (left) and Florence Wyle (right) worked throughout their careers to show people that sculpture is as important as other art forms. Frances was happiest when working on massive statues, while Florence is known for her smaller sculptures of children and animals.

The two artists became known as The Girls and worked in an old Toronto church. It was so cold in winter that Frances and Florence had to work close to the stove so that their plaster forms and clay wouldn't freeze in mid-sculpture.

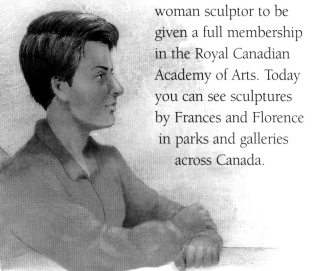

Frances won a number of competitions to create memorials for people who had died during World War I (1914–1918). She also helped found the Sculptors' Society of Canada and worked hard to make the public understand the importance of sculpture. Florence was the first woman sculptor to be given a full membership in the Royal Canadian Academy of Arts. Today you can see sculptures by Frances and Florence in parks and galleries across Canada.

Geneviève Cadieux

Photographer, sculptor, video artist

Born: *July 17, 1955, at Montreal, PQ*

With her large-scale photos, Geneviève Cadieux looks at nature, the human body and the relationships between people. Some of her huge close-ups focus on body image and how the body is put together. One of her works, called *Memory Gap, an Unexpected Beauty*, is a photo of a scar — blown up to about the size of a large bed sheet.

Geneviève started her career with photos and later added sound and video images. Using dialogue in both French and English, as well as figures that seem to reach out of their space, she encourages viewers to react to her work and get involved.

Although Geneviève began by looking at bodies, she has moved to considering the space between people and landscapes. She represents Canada at many international exhibits and is considered one of the country's most important modern artists.

You can see Geneviève Cadieux's work *La Voie Lactée* (The Milky Way), a giant photo of a pair of red lips, on top of the Montreal Museum of Contemporary Arts.

Paraskeva Clark

Painter

Born: *Oct. 28, 1898, at St. Petersburg, Russia*

Died: *Aug. 10, 1986, at Toronto, ON*

One of Canada's most skilled painters of the 1930s and 1940s, Paraskeva Clark created landscapes and still lifes but is best known for her portraits. She was also one of the few artists of the time whose work focused on social issues. Paraskeva painted during the Great Depression (1929–1939), a time when work was scarce and many people experienced poverty. Her paintings look at the gap between rich and poor.

This outspoken and controversial artist also focused on the artist's place in society, people's rights and women's issues. For example, Paraskeva thought a lot about the difficulties she and other women had balancing their careers and their work in the home. During World War II, the National Gallery of Canada appointed Paraskeva to paint the Women's Division of the Armed Forces.

Painting in Canada at about the same time as Paraskeva were Prudence Heward and Lilias Torrance Newton. Both women were known for their paintings of people. Prudence used brilliant colours and strong shapes to create bold portraits. In 1957, Lilias became the first Canadian to paint official portraits of Queen Elizabeth and Prince Philip.

DOCTORS & SCIENTISTS

I t's hard to believe that a little more than 100 years ago, some people thought attending university was unhealthy for young women or that they weren't smart enough for it. As a result, Canadian women couldn't get the education they needed to become doctors or scientists.

Many women simply ignored the negative attitudes about women and learning. Their curiosity about the world and desire to understand it helped them overcome the barriers they faced and encourage other women to join them. Today about 21 per cent of scientists in Canada are female, and more than half of all doctors graduating from medical schools are women.

Maude Abbott

Doctor

Born: *Mar. 18, 1869, at St. Andrews East, PQ (now Saint-André-Est)*

Died: *Sept. 2, 1940, at Montreal, PQ*

Although Maude Abbott was an excellent student, she couldn't train to be a doctor at McGill University — women were not allowed. But Maude wouldn't give up. In 1890 she applied to Bishop's Medical College in Montreal. She was accepted but was often the only woman in the class.

Maude set up medical practice in Montreal in 1897, treating women and children. Her outstanding research papers on heart problems earned her lots of attention. In 1898 McGill University finally decided that it wanted Maude, first as the assistant curator of its medical museum and a year later as its curator. She designed a system for organizing the important collections of body parts that medical students studied. Maude found the heart specimens fascinating.

Maude Abbott set up the International Association of Medical Museums. It's now the International Academy of Pathology, but its letterhead still says, "Founded by Maude Abbott in 1906."

In 1905 the world-famous Canadian doctor William Osler asked Maude to write an article on congenital heart problems (heart defects that people are born with). Her paper gained her international fame, and the information in it saved the lives of many babies.

Towards the end of her career, Maude published an *Atlas of Congenital Heart Disease*. It led to even greater advances in heart surgery and added to Maude's international fame.

Biruté Galdikas

Orangutan expert

Born: *May 10, 1946, at Wiesbaden, Germany*

When Biruté Galdikas was five, she spent hours in a park near her Toronto home observing the wild animals. By high school, she had narrowed her interest to apes, especially orangutans.

At university, Biruté chose anthropology, the study of humans, including their ancestors and relatives (such as apes). In 1971, she went to Borneo, Indonesia, to study orangutans. Leeches, insects and primitive living conditions — nothing stopped Biruté. She was delighted to be finally observing the "red apes" in their natural habitat.

Orangutans are very shy, and at first they threw branches at Biruté to make her go away. But she patiently waited for them to accept her, and over time she succeeded. Eventually, some of the orangutans travelled and ate with her and even slept beside her.

Biruté still spends about half of every year studying orangutans and attempting to protect them from poachers and others who threaten their survival. She is the world's authority on orangutans and started the Orangutan Foundation International.

"I HOPE [I CAN] HELP PEOPLE UNDERSTAND ORANGUTANS AND THEIR TROPICAL RAIN FOREST WORLD, A WORLD WHICH IS IN GRAVE DANGER OF VANISHING FOREVER."

— *Biruté Galdikas*

Harriet Brooks Pitcher

Nuclear physicist

Born: *July 2, 1876, at Exeter, ON*

Died: *Apr. 17, 1933, at Montreal, PQ*

It was unlikely that Harriet Brooks would study science at university. Not only did she live at a time when it was difficult for women to get an education, but she also came from a poor family. However, Harriet was a good student and won scholarships. In 1894 she began studying at McGill University in Montreal.

Harriet graduated in 1898 and a year later began researching radioactivity, a new field in science. She studied radioactive elements (an element is a substance made up of only one kind of atom) and proved that one element could change into another, something scientists had thought impossible. While doing this work, she helped identify the element radon.

In 1903 Harriet discovered that when a radioactive atom ejects a particle, the atom springs back, or recoils. This became known as the "recoil theory" of atoms and is still important today. From 1906 to 1907, she worked with Marie Curie who was then the only woman physicist more famous than Harriet.

Harriet married Frank Pitcher in 1907, and, as with many women at

the time, marriage ended her work in science. But she had accomplished more during her short career than many scientists do in a lifetime.

James Barry

Doctor

Born: *around 1795, at London, England*

Died: *1865, at London, England*

In the early 1800s, women couldn't study medicine or even attend university. What could a woman do who wanted to be a doctor? Disguise herself!

James Barry was a bad-tempered British Army surgeon who flirted with ladies, fought a duel and was always seen with a black poodle. Only 1.5 m (5 ft.) tall and very feminine looking, James performed difficult operations with great skill. Soldiers loved the

eccentric doctor because James insisted on better food for them and improved their hospitals.

After serving in South Africa and the Caribbean, James came to Canada in 1857 as inspector general of military hospitals (the army's top doctor in Canada). In 1859 James became ill but refused to be examined and was sent home to England. James died a few years later, and that's when the doctor's secret was discovered: James was a woman!

Who had James Barry really been? No one knows for sure. Some think her name was Miss Bulkeley and that a male relative helped her get into medical school. Although she was in Canada only for two years, she was the first woman to work as a doctor here, and the discovery after her death brought her incredible fame.

Irene Ayako Uchida

Geneticist

Born: *Apr. 8, 1917, at Vancouver, BC*

Genetics is the science that deals with heredity. A scientist who studies a cell's chromosomes, the thin strands of genes that contain all the hereditary information, is called a cytogeneticist. Dr. Irene Ayako Uchida was one of the first Canadians to work in this field and became a world-famous cytogeneticist.

In the 1960s, Irene discovered that pregnant women who were x-rayed were more likely to give birth to children with Down Syndrome, which results in mental disabilities. She also analysed chromosomes to predict disorders caused by genes.

"Science is a rewarding and challenging career," Irene says. Young people going into science must keep an open mind to all ideas in an effort to find every possible way to help people." She believes that some day geneticists may be able to deactivate certain genes before babies are born and so cure some genetic diseases.

DID YOU KNOW

Irene Uchida wanted to be a social worker. But one of her professors was so impressed with her work in a genetics course that she persuaded Irene to change her mind.

Emily Stowe

Doctor and suffragist

Born: May 1, 1831, at Norwich, ON

Died: Apr. 30, 1903, at Toronto, ON

Like other women who tried to study medicine in Canada more than 100 years ago, Emily Jennings Stowe found the doors of Canadian universities closed. She was definitely smart enough — in 1852 she'd become Canada's first woman school principal. So Emily went to the United States and graduated as a doctor in 1867. That still didn't allow her to practise medicine legally back home, but she opened an office in Toronto anyway.

In the early 1870s, Emily and another woman, Jennie Trout, were reluctantly admitted to the Toronto School of Medicine to complete their studies. The professors and students made the women's lives difficult, but in 1880 Emily was given a doctor's licence to work in Ontario. (Jenny had earned hers in 1875, becoming the first woman to receive a medical licence in Canada.)

To make it easier for other women to become doctors, Emily opened the Woman's Medical

College in 1878. Emily's daughter, Augusta Stowe-Gullen, was so inspired by her mother that in 1883 she graduated from the Toronto School of Medicine — the first woman to take her entire medical training in Canada.

Frances McGill

Crime investigator

Born: Nov. 18, 1882, at Minnedosa, MB

Died: Jan. 21, 1959, at Winnipeg, MB

Dead bodies, poison, bloodstains — Frances McGill dealt with them all, and more. She started university studying law but switched to medicine and became a doctor. In 1922 she became Saskatchewan's Provincial Pathologist, the province's expert on diseases.

As a pathologist, Frances also worked with the Royal Canadian Mounted Police (RCMP) to investigate suspicious deaths. It was gruelling and sometimes gruesome work. Occasionally, she had to travel long distances by dogsled or float plane to examine a crime scene. Frances often had a stronger stomach than the Mounties working with her. She once told a constable, "Pull yourself together, you sissy!"

Frances helped solve hundreds of murder cases. RCMP officers respected and admired her, and she earned the nickname Saskatchewan Sherlock Holmes. She was a good witness in court trials, and the evidence she presented was always considered useful and important.

In 1946, Frances was made Honorary Surgeon to the RCMP, the only woman ever given this title.

Frances McGill has a lake named after her: McGill Lake in Saskatchewan, north of Lake Athabasca.

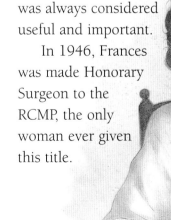

Leonora King

Doctor

Born: Mar. 17, 1851, at Farmersville (now Athens), ON

Died: June 30, 1925, at Tientsin (now Tianjin), China

When being a woman prevented Leonora Howard from studying medicine in Canada, she headed to the United States. In 1876 she graduated from medical school and a year later sailed to China as a medical missionary to spread Christianity and care for the sick. She became the first Canadian doctor in China.

Leonora worked tirelessly, and her efforts helped make foreigners more accepted in China. Treating poor women and children was her focus, but she also cared for royals — then persuaded them to fund clinics and hospitals.

In 1884 Leonora married Alexander King and continued living in China. For her work with wounded soldiers during the 1894–1895 war with Japan, she was awarded the Imperial Order of the Double Dragon. She was the first non-Asian woman to receive this high honour.

To train doctors and nurses, Leonora set up a government

medical school for women in 1908. She worked in China for 47 years, saving lives and improving the health of thousands.

Ursula Franklin

Physicist and peace activist

Born: Sept. 16, 1921, at Munich, Germany

As an expert on metals, Ursula Franklin used her knowledge in a number of ways. She was one of the first to apply modern techniques to analyse ancient artifacts and discover their age, where they were made and more. She also gathered and examined data on radioactive material in Canadian children's teeth. (The radioactive material was a result of nuclear weapons testing.)

While a student during World War II, Ursula had been imprisoned in a Nazi work camp. That experience made her value peace and campaign against war. Ever since then, she has spoken out against nuclear weapons

and has raised awareness about conflict resolution. Her efforts won her Canada's Pearson Peace Medal in 2002.

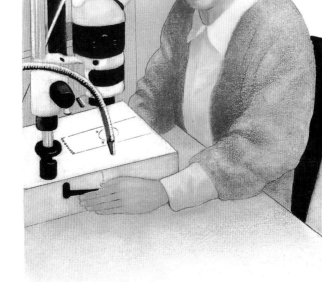

"I HAVE VERY STRONGLY MADE THE POINT THROUGHOUT MY LIFE THAT PEACE IS THE ONLY WAY IN WHICH A CIVILIZATION CAN CONTINUE AND THRIVE."

— *Ursula Franklin*

Ursula believes that women have a lot to offer the world of science. She feels that women ask different questions than men ask and bring more of a spirit of cooperation to the field.

Helen Sawyer Hogg

Astronomer

Born: *Aug. 1, 1905, at Lowell, MA*

Died: *Jan. 28, 1993, at Toronto, ON*

"I was nearly a chemist, but the total eclipse of the sun on January 24, 1925, changed my mind." That's how Helen Sawyer Hogg explained her love of astronomy (the study of stars, planets and galaxies). In 1931, she received a doctorate in astronomy from Radcliffe College in Boston, MA.

That same year, Helen and her astronomer husband, Frank Hogg, moved to Saanich, British Columbia, because Frank got a job at the observatory there. Helen did volunteer work at the observatory but only when Frank was there, too — it was considered improper for Helen to be alone with male workers.

Helen and Frank moved to Toronto, and in 1936 she began teaching at the University of Toronto. She became a world expert on globular star clusters, groups of stars that are the oldest objects in our Milky Way galaxy. Her work also led to the discovery that new stars are constantly formed.

Getting ordinary people interested in the stars was important to Helen, and she wrote a book and many articles sharing her love of astronomy. She earned many honours in her career, including being the first woman president of both the Royal Astronomical Society of Canada and the Royal Canadian Institute. She was also the first president of the Canadian Astronomical Society.

Minor planet No. 2917, between Jupiter and Mars, was renamed "Sawyer Hogg" in honour of Helen Sawyer Hogg in 1984.

Alice Wilson

Geologist and palaeontologist

Born: *Aug. 26, 1881, at Cobourg, ON*

Died: *Apr. 15, 1964, at Ottawa, ON*

Not only did Alice Wilson's parents emphasize learning, they also encouraged their children to enjoy the outdoors. No wonder Alice became Canada's first female geologist, a scientist who studies the origin, history and structure of Earth.

In 1909 Alice joined the Geological Survey of Canada, an organization that gathers information on Canada's rocks and minerals. A few years later, she also began a career in palaeontology, the study of prehistoric life. Alice faced many obstacles as a woman in these sciences. For instance, the Geological Survey wouldn't issue her a car for field trips, as it did for men. She had to buy her own so that she could continue her research.

Alice became a world-recognized expert on the rocks of the Ottawa area. Although she always suffered from poor health, she was still enthusiastically leading trips for students when she was in her eighties. She felt it was important that ordinary people, especially children, understand geology. Alice also worked to have women's contributions to the sciences and other fields recognized.

WRITERS

The first person in Canada to sell one million copies of a book was a woman. Margaret Marshall Saunders's children's story *Beautiful Joe* was published in 1894 and is still read by kids today. Look for it in your local library or bookstore.

By the early 1900s, hundreds of women in Canada were writing books. It's hard to know the exact number: some felt they had to use men's names to be accepted. Today Canadian women writers proudly use their own names, and many of them are famous around the world.

Lucy Maud Montgomery

Children's writer

Born: *Nov. 30, 1874, at Clifton (now New London), PE*

Died: *Apr. 24, 1942, at Toronto, ON*

When Lucy Maud Montgomery received *The Daily Patriot* newspaper on November 26, 1890, she was thrilled. There was her poem! She was just 16, and she had been published for the first time.

Maud kept writing poems and short stories, even while working as a teacher or in a newspaper office. By 1905 she'd given up her other jobs and was focusing on her writing. But she still had never written a book.

One day Maud was looking through an old notebook filled with ideas for stories. She found a note she'd written earlier: "Elderly couple apply to orphan asylum for a boy. By mistake a girl is sent them." Immediately, Maud imagined what this girl was like. Her name even popped into Maud's head: Anne-with-an-e. Maud liked her character so much that she decided to write a book about her.

While washing dishes or hanging laundry, Maud worked out plot and dialogue. She finished the manuscript in October 1905 and sent it to a publisher — who quickly sent it back. After the fifth rejection, Maud sadly put her book away. Months later, while cleaning out a cupboard, she came across it and decided to try once more. Finally, it was accepted!

That book, *Anne of Green Gables*, has been published in more than 20 languages and has sold tens of millions of copies. Maud wrote many other books, and some have been made into movies, musicals, plays and television shows. Although Maud's first book is now about 100 years old, it's still a bestseller and a Canadian classic with fans all over the world.

"I CANNOT REMEMBER THE TIME WHEN I WAS NOT WRITING, OR WHEN I DID NOT MEAN TO BE AN AUTHOR."

— *Lucy Maud Montgomery*

Margaret Atwood

Novelist and poet

Born: Nov. 18, 1939, at Ottawa, ON

Talk about versatile — Margaret Atwood has written poems, children's stories, novels and short stories. Her work has been made into plays, TV shows, movies and even an opera.

Margaret published her first book, a volume of poetry, in 1961. Five years later, when she was just 27, her second book of poetry, *The Circle Game*, won the Governor

General's Literary Award. Margaret began writing novels in 1969 and 16 years later won a second Governor General's Award for her book *The Handmaid's Tale*.

Human rights are important to Margaret, and she has worked for many years with Amnesty International. This organization strives to free people who have been unjustly imprisoned because of their beliefs. Fighting censorship of writers is also a priority for her.

Margaret has set her stories in the past, present and even the future. Her writing has been translated into more than 25 languages, and she has won literary prizes around the world.

Margaret Murray

Newspaper publisher

Born: Aug. 3, 1888, at Windy Ridges, KS, U.S.

Died: Sept. 25, 1982, at Lillooet, BC

Some people loved her and other people hated her, but Margaret "Ma" Murray always got a reaction. She published outspoken editorials and articles and changed how people thought about newspapers and women journalists.

It was Ma's husband, George, who got her involved in publishing. He ran a number of newspapers in British Columbia. But when he got interested in politics, Ma found herself doing more and more work on the newspapers.

Ma's newspaper articles weren't always grammatical, and the swear words in them irritated some readers. But she would take on any subject,

DID YOU KNOW

The masthead of one of Ma Murray's papers, the *Bridge River-Lillooet News*, said: "Printed in the Sagebrush Country of the Lillooet every Thursday, God willing. Guarantees a chuckle every week and a belly laugh once a month or your money back."

whether economics, morals or politics. Sometimes her opinions were so forceful they led to lawsuits. As her articles were reprinted across Canada, Ma's fame grew. Today her name stands for independent thinking and candid speech.

Pauline Johnson

Poet, Aboriginal rights activist and entertainer

Born: Mar. 10, 1861, on the Six Nations Indian Reserve at Ohsweken, ON

Died: Mar. 7, 1913, at Vancouver, BC

A hundred years ago, Emily Pauline Johnson was Canada's most popular entertainer. She toured Canada, Britain and the United States, reading her poetry and talking about Canada and Aboriginal rights. Billing herself as the Mohawk Princess because her father was a Mohawk chief, she called herself Tekahionwake (you say it Dega-hee-yawn-wagay), which means "double wampum" in Mohawk.

Pauline began writing poetry when she was a child. However, she wasn't much of a success as a poet until she gave a reading of her work and performed it with great flair. To emphasize her Aboriginal heritage, she wore a buckskin with two human scalps hanging from her waist. People swarmed to see her, even though they were sometimes shocked when she demanded better treatment for Aboriginal people.

The first Aboriginal poet published in Canada, Pauline was also one of the few female writers of the time who could make a living writing and performing. She's also the only person buried in Stanley Park, which was her favourite place in Vancouver.

"MY AIM, MY JOY, MY PRIDE IS TO SING THE GLORIES OF MY OWN PEOPLE."

— *Pauline Johnson*

Gabrielle Roy

Novelist

Born: Mar. 22, 1909, at St-Boniface, MB

Died: July 13, 1983, at Quebec, PQ

Imagine having your first book win some of the world's most important prizes! That's what Gabrielle Roy did. Her novel *Bonheur d'occasion* (translated as *The Tin Flute*) won the Governor General's Literary Award in 1947, the Literary Guild of America Award and the Prix Fémina from France. It was the first time this French award had gone to a foreign author.

A brilliant student in her youth, Gabrielle did not go to university. Her family was too poor to send her. She became a teacher, then an actor and later a journalist and novelist. Gabrielle's prairie background influenced her writing, as did the life stories of the immigrants who had come to western Canada. In her simple, straightforward way, she examined people's loneliness and hope for a better world.

Gabrielle went on to win more prizes, including a total of three Governor General's Literary Awards. She also wrote three books for children and was the first woman elected into the Royal Society of Canada, a group of Canada's most important artists and scientists.

Alice Munro

Short-story writer

Born: July 10, 1931, at Wingham, ON

Canada's most famous short-story author, Alice Munro, started writing stories when she was 12. At first she wrote adventure stories — often with herself as the hero. She began by writing in the style of other writers, but gradually developed her own distinctive voice.

Alice writes about ordinary people and situations, painting intense word-pictures of how people think and behave. Many of her stories look at the lives of women, from teenage girls to middle-aged women and seniors. She describes her writing as "autobiographical in form, but not in fact."

Very skilled at writing dialogue, Alice is also extremely insightful and observant. Because of this, she can create such realistic characters

DID YOU KNOW

Most of Alice Munro's stories take place in Huron County, Ontario, where she lives.

that it's easy for readers to see themselves in her stories.

A lot of care goes into Alice's work — she often writes and re-writes over and over, making small but important changes. All of this effort has paid off: Alice has won many prizes around the world for her writing, including winning the Governor General's Literary Award three times.

Ella Cora Hind

Journalist

Born: Sept. 18, 1861, at Toronto, ON

Died: Oct. 6, 1942, at Winnipeg, MB

"A newspaper office is no place for a woman!" That's what Ella Cora Hind heard in 1882 when she applied for a job at the *Manitoba Free Press* in Winnipeg. So instead she learned to type — the typewriter was still a new invention — and became Manitoba's first typist. A year later, she opened her own typing office.

But Cora still wanted to be a journalist. In 1901 the *Free Press* finally changed its mind and hired her. At that time, women journalists were expected to write about "women's" subjects, such as fashion or cooking. However, Cora had always been fascinated by farming and was made the agricultural editor. Within a few years she was famous for her incredibly accurate predictions — usually off by no more than 1 per cent — of the western Canadian wheat crop yield.

One of the first woman journalists in the West, Cora also worked with rural women and with Nellie McClung (page 6) to get women the vote in Manitoba. That happened in 1916. But Cora never lost interest in farming. Even when she was 75, she travelled the world to observe new methods of agriculture.

Carol Shields

Novelist, poet, playwright

Born: *June 2, 1935, at Oak Park, IL, U.S.*

Died: *July 16, 2003, at Victoria, BC*

The details and humour of everyday life and the difficulty of truly knowing another person are all part of Carol Shields's writing. She also found intriguing the cross-overs between fiction, biography and autobiography. For instance, in Carol's first novel, *Small Ceremonies*, published in 1976, the main character is writing about Susanna Moodie (see below), just as Carol did for a university paper. That book went on to win awards, as have many of her other books.

It was while Carol was raising her family of five that she began writing. She used to steal away time to write, sometimes as little as an hour a day. Her novels were very short then, she joked. Carol could write almost anywhere — even on family car trips she would scribble away in her notebook.

Carol's book *The Stone Diaries*, published in 1993, was probably her most famous, winning the Governor General's Literary Award and the Pulitzer Prize, one of the top American awards for writing.

> "I DRIFTED INTO WRITING FICTION. I CERTAINLY NEVER SET OUT WITH A PLAN FOR A CAREER PATH. WITH FIVE CHILDREN, I WAS JUST TOO BUSY."
>
> — *Carol Shields*

Susanna Moodie and Catharine Parr Traill

Pioneer authors

Susanna Moodie

Born: *Dec. 6, 1803, at Bungay, England*

Died: *Apr. 8, 1885, at Toronto, ON*

Catharine Parr Traill

Born: *Jan. 9, 1802, at London, England*

Died: *Aug. 29, 1899, at Lakefield, ON*

When sisters Susanna Moodie (left) and Catharine Parr Traill (right) became famous writers, their family couldn't have been surprised. After all, three of their four sisters were writers. But Susanna and Catharine earned their fame by writing about Canada, where they emigrated from England in 1832.

They wrote about their lives as settlers in 1836, Catharine published *The Backwoods of Canada* a collection of letters and diary entries. In 1852, Susanna published *Roughing It in the Bush*, which humorously described life in the wilderness. Today, the sisters' books provide useful information about pioneer times. And Susanna, in particular, has inspired many Canadian writers, including Margaret Atwood (page 41) and Carol Shields (above).

In 1852 Catharine wrote the first Canadian adventure novel for kids, *Canadian Crusoes*, which is still available in libraries and bookstores. As well, her books about plants in Upper Canada were read by scientists worldwide. The books were illustrated by one of Susanna's daughters, who had been taught by her talented mother.

Margaret Laurence

Novelist

Born: *July 18, 1926, at Neepawa, MB*

Died: *Jan. 5, 1987, at Lakefield, ON*

At age seven, Jean Margaret Wemyss began writing. She continued to do so throughout school, but it wasn't until she married John Laurence and moved to Africa in 1950 that she began to write seriously. When the family returned to Canada in 1957, she focused on writing about her own country.

Five of Margaret's most famous books take place in the town of Manawaka, Manitoba, a made-up place based on her hometown of Neepawa. Of these, *A Jest of God* (1966) and *The Diviners* (1974) won Governor General's Literary Awards. These books look at life in a small

prairie town, as well as the conflict between fitting into society and being an individual. Margaret also wrote four books for children.

A good ear for dialogue and sensitivity to those cut off from society are two of the things that make Margaret's writing so powerful. She used her fame to raise awareness of the environment, peace and literacy.

DID YOU KNOW

You can visit the Margaret Laurence Home in Neepawa, Manitoba, where Margaret grew up. There you can see her typewriter, awards and more.

Antonine Maillet

Acadian writer

Born: *May 10, 1929, at Bouctouche, NB*

Antonine Maillet is an Acadian, a descendant of French-speaking Maritimers who were forced off their land by the British, starting in 1755. The "expulsion of the Acadians" almost destroyed Acadian culture, and little was known about Acadia outside the area even into the 1900s.

As a child, Antonine was fascinated by Acadia and became determined to write about it. "I was very aware that I had to write

something that had never been written before," she says. "I knew I could not let the voice of my people die without a last cry." She learned the skill of storytelling by listening to her relatives, by learning Acadian

folklore and from village entertainers.

La Sagouine, published in 1971, tells the story of an Acadian charlady, using the unique Acadian dialect. The novel was turned into a play, and it made Antonine and actress Viola Léger famous in both English and French Canada.

In 1972, Antonine won the Governor General's Literary Award for *Don l'Orignal*. Seven years later she became the first person outside France to win the Prix Goncourt, France's most important literary award, for the novel *Pélagie-la-Charette* (or *Pélagie: The Return to a Homeland*). "I have avenged my ancestors," said Antonine.

POLITICIANS & LAWMAKERS

Canadian women couldn't vote in federal elections until May 24, 1918. Being able to vote was an important step forward, and gradually women began to enter politics and the law.

Today, male politicians and judges still outnumber females, and politics and lawmaking can be tough careers for women. Charlotte Whitton, mayor of Ottawa in the mid-1900s, said, "Whatever women do they must do twice as well as men to be thought half as good." Then she added, "Luckily, this is not difficult."

Nellie Cournoyea

> **Territorial leader**
>
> **Born:** Mar. 4, 1940, at Aklavik, NT

When someone in Inuvik, Northwest Territories, says, "You'd better ask Nellie," everyone knows he means Nellie Cournoyea. She is one of the most powerful women in northern Canada, because she understands both Inuit culture and big business.

Nellie grew up in the traditional way of her people, the Inuvialuit of the Mackenzie Delta. Her family travelled and hunted on the shore of the Beaufort Sea. By the time she was eight, Nellie was interested in politics and had the job of recording what was said at community meetings.

During the 1960s, Nellie worked for CBC radio in Inuvik. She fought to get money for shows that reflected Inuit culture. In the 1970s, she was hard at work negotiating Aboriginal land claims.

Elected to the Northwest Territories legislature in 1979, Nellie held such jobs as Minister of Health and Social Services, Minister of Energy, Mines and Petroleum Resources, Minister of Public Works and Highways and more.

When she was elected to lead the Northwest Territories in 1991, Nellie became the first Native woman elected premier in Canada. Her territory was one-fifth the size of the whole country! With a focus on reducing administration, Nellie shifted money and responsibility to community leaders who knew what was needed in their areas.

Stepping down as premier in 1995, Nellie became head of the Inuvialuit Regional Corporation, which manages lands and money she helped negotiate in the 1984 land claim. Nellie continues to work hard to help her people determine their own future.

DID YOU KNOW

For high school, Nellie Cournoyea had correspondence courses flown up from Alberta to her family's trapline.

Agnes Macphail

Member of Parliament

Born: *Mar. 24, 1890, at Grey County, ON*

Died: *Feb. 13, 1954, at Toronto, ON*

Canada's federal election of 1921 was the first in which women could vote and be elected. There were four women candidates but only one succeeded: Agnes Macphail. She was in Parliament for almost 20 years. For the first 14 years, she was the only woman.

Agnes focused on agriculture, as well as pensions, prison conditions and other social issues. But most people didn't want to listen to Agnes — they wanted to gawk at her because she was the only woman in Parliament. Some people criticized her for not wearing a hat in the House of Commons.

"I was a curiosity, a freak," said Agnes, but peoples' prejudices did not stop her. In 1929 she became the first Canadian woman in the League of Nations (it came before the United Nations). She also founded the Canadian Elizabeth Fry Society to help women and girls in the justice system.

When Agnes lost in the 1940 federal election, she switched to Ontario politics and was elected in 1943 and 1948. She was responsible for the province's first laws to have women paid the same as men.

Roberta Jamieson

Aboriginal activist

Born: *Oct. 10, 1953, on Six Nations of the Grand River Reserve (near Brantford, ON)*

Roberta Jamieson's life is full of firsts: first Aboriginal woman to become a lawyer in Canada (in 1976), first woman ombudsman (a provincial official who investigates complaints against the government by citizens) in Ontario (1989) and first woman chief of the Six Nations of the Grand River (2001).

Probably best known for her negotiating skills, Roberta learned and practised her techniques within her large family. Her methods of conflict resolution help support and assist both sides, and experts in Asia, Africa, Europe and North America have all asked for her assistance.

A dynamic Mohawk leader, Roberta works hard for better relations between government and Aboriginal peoples. Passion, problem-solving skills and willingness to take risks are all qualities she brings to her job as chief of the reserve with the largest population in Canada.

"... IN MY CULTURE, WOMEN HAVE ALWAYS PLAYED THE ROLE OF FACILITATING AGREEMENT, WHETHER IT WAS AT THE DINNER TABLE OR ELSEWHERE. IN OUR CULTURE, WOMEN ARE THE CONSCIENCE OF THE COUNCIL, OF THE CHIEFS."

— *Roberta Jamieson*

Jean Augustine

Member of Parliament

Born: *Sept. 9, 1937, at St. George's, Grenada*

Secretary of State for Multiculturalism and the Status of Women. In 1995 Jean helped have February designated Black History Month across Canada.

Like Member of Parliament Agnes Macphail (page 47), Jean Augustine was a school principal before she got into politics. She was also the national president of the Congress of Black Women of Canada.

Soon after becoming the first Black woman elected to Parliament in 1993, Jean was made Parliamentary Secretary (special assistant) to the Prime Minister. She then served as

Social issues in particular concern Jean. She works hard to improve the lives of young Canadians and supports the Jean Augustine Scholarship Fund, which helps single mothers studying at a Toronto college.

"… RACISM IS THE UNDERLYING CORE OF THE ADVERSITIES WE FACE AS A PEOPLE. IT IS DEMORALIZING FOR THE ADULTS IN OUR COMMUNITY, AND IT IS ABSOLUTELY DAMAGING TO OUR YOUTH."

— *Jean Augustine*

Cairine Wilson

Senator

Born: *Feb. 4, 1885, at Montreal, PQ*

Died: *Mar. 3, 1962, at Ottawa, ON*

There was a lot of opposition when, in 1930, Cairine Wilson became the first Canadian woman appointed to the Senate. Most people thought Prime Minister William Lyon Mackenzie King should have chosen Emily Murphy (page 6) instead

"IT HAS BEEN A GREAT JOY AND SATISFACTION TO ME TO KNOW, AND TO BE ASSURED BY MY COLLEAGUES OF MY OWN SEX, THAT I MADE THE WAY MORE EASY FOR THEM."

— *Cairine Wilson*

because of her work to have women declared eligible to become senators. As well, the other senators, all men, didn't want a woman in the Senate.

Cairine suspected that, in return for her appointment, the Prime Minister (PM) would expect her to go along with his government's proposals. But Cairine was tough and wasn't afraid to disagree with him.

As chairman of the Canadian National Committee on Refugees from 1938 to 1948, Cairine worked hard on behalf of refugees and immigrants. Her interest in people from other countries lead her to be appointed Canada's first woman delegate to the United Nations, in 1949.

But she is best known for her ground-breaking role as a senator. Thanks to pioneers such as Cairine, today about a third of Canada's senators are women. That's one of the highest percentages in similar assemblies anywhere in the world.

Thérèse Casgrain

Reformer

Born: *July 10, 1896, at Montreal, PQ*

Died: *Nov. 3, 1981, at Montreal, PQ*

By 1925, women in all ten provinces could vote in provincial elections — except the women of Quebec. For years they had campaigned for the vote with no success. Eventually, it was decided they'd do better with a single representative, and Marie Thérèse Forget Casgrain was chosen to lead the fight to reform the voting law. The struggle lasted until 1940 when, finally, the women of Quebec were allowed to vote.

After this success, Thérèse turned her attention to other social issues, such as child protection and prison reform, and fought to ban nuclear weapons. In 1951 she was chosen head of the Co-operative Commonwealth Federation (later the

In 1912, young Thérèse Forget (later Casgrain) and her parents were scheduled to sail home from Paris. Luckily, her father's business delayed them, and they missed their ship, the doomed *Titanic*.

New Democratic Party) in Quebec, becoming the first woman ever to lead a political party in Canada.

In 1970 Thérèse joined Canada's Senate. However, she had to leave the next year at age 75, the mandatory retirement age. But retirement didn't silence Thérèse. She continued to campaign for charities and consumers' rights — and against enforced retirement.

Bertha Wilson

Supreme Court judge

Born: *Sept. 18, 1923, in Kirkcaldy, Scotland*

The Supreme Court was established in 1875. It's Canada's highest court — if a Canadian doesn't agree with a decision made by another court, he or she can take the case to the Supreme Court. It took more than 100 years for a woman to be appointed a Supreme Court judge, but in 1982 Bertha Wilson achieved that honour.

Bertha had already been the first

woman appointed to Ontario's highest court, the Ontario Court of Appeal, in 1975. There, she became known as a legal innovator, famous for her creative decisions in human rights, discrimination and child custody cases. Her decisions were controversial but showed a deep understanding of law.

Bertha served on Canada's Supreme Court until 1991, and her writings about Canada's laws are still some of the most frequently used by the court. In 1996 she contributed to the Royal Commission on Aboriginal People. But women's issues continue to be a special interest. "Women lawyers and women judges, through their differing perspectives on life," believes Bertha, "can bring a new humanity to bear on the decision-making process."

Jeanne Sauvé

Governor General

Born: *Apr. 26, 1922, at Prud'homme, SK*

Died: *Jan. 26, 1993, at Montreal, PQ*

When Jeanne-Mathilde Sauvé became Canada's first woman Governor General in 1983, she said it was "a magnificent breakthrough for women." But it wasn't the only first in Jeanne's life.

In 1972 Jeanne had become the first Quebec woman appointed to the federal Cabinet (a group of advisors to the Prime Minister). In 1980 she'd been made the first female Speaker of the House of Commons. (The Speaker not only keeps order during debates in the House of Commons but also manages expenses and staff for the House.) Jeanne revamped the operation, saving $18 million — and improving services. During her time as a Member of Parliament, she also opened the first daycare centre on Parliament Hill.

As Governor General, Jeanne focused on national unity, peace and youth. She started the Jeanne Sauvé Youth Foundation to motivate young people and set up the Jeanne Sauvé Trophy for the world cup championship in women's field hockey.

Since Jeanne's term as Governor General, Adrienne Clarkson and Michaëlle Jean have also been appointed to the position.

Rosemary Brown

Provincial politician

Born: *June 17, 1930, at Kingston, Jamaica*

Died: *Apr. 26, 2003, at Vancouver, BC*

When Rosemary Brown arrived in Canada from Jamaica in 1950, no one would be her roommate. Why? Because she was Black. Later, she found it difficult to get a job or find a place to live. "To be Black and female in a society which is both racist and sexist," Rosemary once said, "is to be in the unique position of having nowhere to go but up!"

When Rosemary was approached to be a political candidate, she was sure she'd lose — but she won! From 1972 to 1986, she was a Member of the Legislative Assembly of British Columbia, the first Black woman elected to political office in Canada.

"WOMEN SHOULD ENTER POLITICS TO BRING ABOUT CHANGE. IT'S A TOUGH ARENA ... THE SACRIFICES CALLED FOR CAN BE ONLY JUSTIFIED ON THE GROUNDS THAT WE ARE INDEED MAKING THE WORLD, OR OUR COMMUNITY, A BETTER PLACE ..."

— *Rosemary Brown*

Rosemary was also the first woman in Canada to run for the leadership of a national political party, the New Democratic Party. She lost in a close race, but her attempt encouraged many women to become involved in politics.

Audrey McLaughlin

Federal political party leader

Born: *Nov. 7, 1936, at Dutton, ON*

Social worker, teacher, mink farmer — Audrey McLaughlin was all of these before going into politics. In 1979, she drove from Toronto to Whitehorse, Yukon Territory, looking for adventure.

Audrey soon became active in politics and, in 1987, was elected to

"… THE WORLD HAS BECOME INCREASINGLY COMPLEX AND INTERDEPENDENT AND WE CAN NO LONGER AFFORD TO IGNORE THE SKILLS AND EXPERTISE OF HALF OF THE WORLD'S POPULATION."

— *Audrey McLaughlin*

Canada's House of Commons. That made her the first New Democratic Party (NDP) Member of Parliament ever elected in Yukon. Just two years later she became the first woman to lead a national Canadian political party when she was elected leader of the NDP.

The 1990s were a time of great change in Canadian politics, and it was tough being a party leader. But Audrey was determined, especially about giving Aboriginal peoples, northerners and women more say in federal politics. When she stepped down as leader of the NDP in 1995, she was replaced by another woman, Alexa McDonough.

Ellen Fairclough

Cabinet minister

Born: *Jan. 28, 1905, at Hamilton, ON*

Died: *Nov. 13, 2004, at Hamilton, ON*

When Ellen Fairclough entered politics in 1945, she joined the race for city council in Hamilton, Ontario — and lost by three votes. "No one can ever tell me," she said, "that a single vote does not count!"

Eventually, Ellen was elected to council, then in 1950 moved to federal politics, where she became known as a human rights supporter. She pushed for women to receive the same opportunities and pay as men.

In 1957 Ellen was the first woman appointed to the Cabinet. When Prime Minister John Diefenbaker went travelling in 1958, he made Ellen the Acting Prime

Minister of Canada. Although she held the position for less than two days, it signalled women's growing importance in politics.

As Minister of Citizenship and Immigration, Ellen was responsible for Aboriginal people's concerns and in 1960 got legislation passed giving them the vote in federal elections. She brought in regulations in 1962 to stop discrimination against immigrants based on their colour, race or home country. Throughout her career, Ellen also encouraged women to take part in politics.

ATHLETES

omen athletes? Not possible! Females are too frail and delicate for sports. That's what people said 100 years ago. But thanks to pioneering Canadian women, such as the ones you'll read about here, girls and women now take part in many sports.

Experts say women athletes are improving faster than men. Some sports analysts think that in 150 years or so, the world's fastest runner, for example, may be a woman. Who knows — she may even be a woman proudly wearing Canada's red maple leaf on her uniform!

Nancy Greene

Skier

Born: *May 11, 1943, at Ottawa, ON*

As Nancy Greene skied down the giant slalom course at the 1968 Olympic Winter Games, she knew she was having her best race ever. But when she got to the bottom, strange numbers that made no sense appeared on the timing clock. Was the clock broken? Had it missed timing Nancy?

The clock was working just fine — Nancy's time was so much faster than anyone else's that it had to be confirmed before it could be shown. She won gold by one of the largest margins in Olympic history.

Nancy had always been fast. Her aggressive style earned her the nickname Tiger. It also caused her torn ligaments, a dislocated shoulder and a broken leg. Although she didn't begin serious racing until she was 14, just two years later she was fast enough to make the 1960 Olympic team. But Nancy only finished 22nd in her event, the giant slalom. She wasn't discouraged. She realized she had to make some changes.

Nancy knew she needed to ski with more control, without losing speed. Years of hard work followed, and then some big wins. During the 1966–1967 ski season she became the first North American skier to win the World Cup. The Cup was hers the next year as well, when she won ten races in a row. At the 1968 Olympics, she also won a silver medal to go with her incredible gold.

No Canadian skier has won as many medals as Nancy did. Because of this, she was named the greatest Canadian female athlete of the twentieth century.

"I LEARNED THAT I COULD COME UP WITH BETTER RESULTS AND MORE CONSISTENT FINISHES ... IF I REALLY CONCENTRATED ON A COURSE INSTEAD OF ALMOST BLINDLY ASSAULTING IT."

— Nancy Greene

Marilyn Bell

Long-distance swimmer

Born: *Nov. 19, 1937, at Toronto, ON*

For years, people had tried to swim across Lake Ontario, but failed. In 1954, American swimmer Florence Chadwick was promised $10 000 if she completed the swim. Some Torontonians thought Canadians should be involved too, so Marilyn Bell and Winnie Roach Leuszler (the first Canadian to swim the English Channel) agreed to swim.

The swimmers had to wait for the best weather and water conditions. Just before midnight on September 8, the time seemed right. The late hour had made Marilyn sleepy, but diving into the frigid water at Youngstown, New York, jolted her awake.

The 16 year old battled high waves, lamprey eels and oil spills. The other two much more experienced swimmers gave up, but Marilyn swam on, at times barely conscious. When she finally reached Toronto almost 21 hours later, she and her coach were shocked to see huge crowds on shore cheering for her.

Marilyn had been motivated by Winnie's success at swimming the English Channel. In turn, Marilyn inspired Vicki Keith, who swam across all five Great Lakes in 1988.

DID YOU KNOW

It took Marilyn Bell about 70 000 strokes to swim Lake Ontario.

Beckie Scott

Cross-country skier

Born: *Aug. 1, 1974, at Vegreville, AB*

It was a race that started on February 15, 2002, and didn't finish until June 25, 2004.

When cross-country skier Becky Scott won a bronze medal in the 5 kilometre free pursuit at the Olympic Winter Games in Salt Lake City, she was excited and happy. It was the first time any Canadian had ever won a medal in cross-country (Nordic) skiing.

But the two women who finished

ahead of Becky tested positive for performance-enhancing drugs in other races. Becky and the Canadian Olympic Committee fought to have

them disqualified. In June 2003 the silver medal was taken from one of the skiers and awarded to Becky. Months later the second racer was disqualified, and Becky got the gold. "This is a precedent-setting moment," she said. "The little guy won out finally ..."

Becky started skiing when she was about four. She wasn't a natural athlete, but her parents encouraged her, and by the time she was 12 she was winning medals at the Canadian Junior nationals. Becky trains hard and works to keep her sport drug-free.

Sandra Schmirler and Colleen Jones

When the first-ever Olympic gold medal for women's curling was awarded in 1998, it went to Sandra Schmirler and her rink (team). Curling with Jan Betker, Joan McCusker and Marcia Gudereit, Sandra won three Canadian Championships and three world titles. Until then, no team made up of the same four women had won more than one world curling title.

An all-round athlete, Sandra was also a fierce competitor. She threw thousands of curling rocks in practice and watched hours of tapes of her performance to see how she could improve. But what people remember most about Sandra is that she really enjoyed her sport and loved her family and friends. When she died of cancer at age 36, the Sandra Schmirler Foundation was set up to help families with seriously ill children.

Another top curler, Colleen Jones has skipped (led) her team to six Canadian Championships and two world titles. When she won the Canadian title in 1982, she was the youngest skip ever to win it. Colleen balances her sport and her career as a sports and weather reporter on national television.

Sandra Schmirler

Colleen Jones

Bobbie Rosenfeld

Tennis, hockey, track, softball — Fanny "Bobbie" Rosenfeld excelled at them all. She won many awards and championships, including gold and silver in track at the 1928 Olympic Games. That was the first year women were allowed to compete at the Olympics. Bobbie scored more points than any other athlete — male or female — and led the small Canadian women's team (nicknamed the Matchless Six) to first place.

Bobbie's sports career started early. While at a picnic as a child, she and her sister lost their lunch money. A kids' race was being held with lunch as the prize. Bobbie was determined to win — and did.

In her early years, Bobbie competed all over Ontario, often wearing her brother's shorts and her dad's socks. She stunned other athletes and wowed fans when she won firsts and seconds in sports she'd never before competed in.

By 1933 severe arthritis ended Bobbie's sports career. She became a sportswriter, known for her wit and strong support of women's rights.

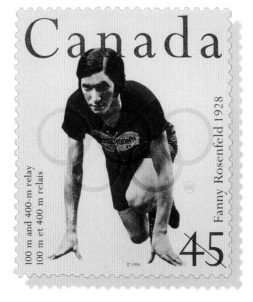

Silken Laumann

Rower

Born: *Nov. 14, 1964, at Mississauga, ON*

"[ROWING] TAUGHT ME HOW TO TAKE RISKS, IT'S TAUGHT ME THAT USUALLY A RISK FEELS SCARY, BUT YOU'VE GOT TO PUSH YOURSELF TO DO IT."

— *Silken Laumann*

While watching the 1976 Olympic Games, 11-year-old Silken Laumann decided she wanted to be a world-class athlete. She was good at track, but her sister, Daniele, a member of Canada's rowing team, encouraged Silken to join her. The sisters won bronze at the Olympics in 1984. Although Daniele quit rowing, Silken continued.

By 1991, Silken was one of the world's best women rowers. Then disaster struck. Just ten weeks before the 1992 Olympics, her boat was accidentally rammed by another boat during training. Her ankle was smashed, and muscles in her leg were shredded. "I actually wondered whether I was going to lose my leg," remembers Silken.

After five operations in ten days, doctors told Silken she would likely never row again. But she wouldn't be stopped. She insisted on being helped from her wheelchair into her boat just 27 days after the accident. With only five weeks to train, Silken amazed the world by winning bronze at the Olympics.

Barbara Ann Scott

Figure skater

Born: *May 9, 1928, at Ottawa, ON*

Until 1947, the World Championships in skating had only been won by Europeans. But that year, Barbara Ann Scott brought the prize home to Canada. She repeated this feat the next year, as well as winning the European Championships and Olympic gold. She was the first North American to win all three in one year.

Barbara Ann started figure skating at age six, and five years later she won the Canadian Junior Championships. Four years after that she became the country's senior champion.

Known for her grace and technique, Barbara Ann was also very competitive and determined. She overcame poor ice conditions and distractions while competing by staying focused. An excellent jumper, she was the first woman ever to land a double Lutz jump in competition.

As Canada's athlete of the year in 1945, 1947 and 1948, Barbara Ann earned the nickname Canada's Sweetheart. She even had a doll named after her. Girls across Canada treasured their Barbara Ann Scott dolls. Her success inspired many Canadian girls to take up skating and motivated such stars as Elizabeth Manley, Karen Magnussen, Shae-Lynn Bourne and Jamie Salé.

Hayley Wickenheiser

Hockey player

Born: Aug. 12, 1978, at Shaunavon, SK

At age five Hayley Wickenheiser joined a boys' hockey team because there were no girls' teams. Other players hit and slashed at her because she was a girl. But she didn't quit — she just scored goals against her tormentors.

In 1993, Hayley became the youngest player ever chosen for Canada's women's hockey team. She was just 15. The team has won many world championships.

At the Olympic Winter Games, the Canadian team won silver in 1998 and gold in 2002. Hayley's contribution to that incredible success is her amazing slap shot and determination. She also competed in the 2000 Olympic Summer Games — as a member of the Canadian softball team.

Although Manon Rhéaume was one of the first women to play men's hockey, Hayley became the first woman to score a point in a men's pro league when she joined Finland's Kirkkonummi Salamat in 2003. Girls and women across the country have been encouraged to play hockey thanks to this international star.

"PEOPLE WOULD SAY, 'GIRLS DON'T PLAY HOCKEY. GIRLS DON'T SKATE.' I WOULD SAY, 'WATCH THIS.' "

— *Hayley Wickenheiser*

Chantal Petitclerc

Track athlete

Born: Dec. 15, 1969, at Saint-Marc-des-Carrières, PQ

Chantal has quick reflexes and is known for her explosive starts. She has great technique and is extremely

"HAPPINESS IS LIKE A MEDAL. IT'S WON BY HOW YOU LIVE EVERY DAY."

— *Chantal Petitclerc*

As a young child, Chantal Petitclerc wasn't an athlete. But when she was 13 an accident left her paralysed from the waist down, and she decided to get involved in sports to stay in shape. Chantal tried swimming, but a track coach noticed her determination and suggested she switch to wheelchair racing. She soon won medals at the Paralympic Games, including gold in all five events in which she competed at the 2004 Games.

competitive. "Don't be afraid to fail sometimes," she says. "Failure, after all, is what gives value to success."

In addition to training four hours a day for her sport, Chantal is also a television host. "I think I project a good image, a dynamic image," she says. "I'm good at my job, and it just so happens that I'm also in a wheelchair." Chantal also campaigns hard to have wheelchair racing recognized as an official sport at the Olympic Games.

The Edmonton Grads

"The finest basketball team that ever stepped out on a floor," is how Dr. James Naismith, basketball's inventor, described Edmonton's Commercial Graduates Basketball Club. No wonder: they had a record of 502 wins and just 20 losses.

What started out as a high-school team dominated women's basketball in North America and Europe for 25 years. Each Grads player was a skilled athlete and dedicated to the game. The team (shown here with their coach) was known for its sense of fair play.

Women's basketball wasn't a medal sport at the Olympic Games when the Grads were dazzling the world. But they represented Canada in exhibition competitions at four Olympic Games held between 1924 and 1936 — and won all 27 matches they played.

The Grads won not only 49 Canadian Championships but also 16 World Championships in a row. Their record makes them the most successful team in any sport in Canadian history.

DID YOU KNOW

The Edmonton Grads went several seasons in a row without losing, stringing together a 146-game winning streak.

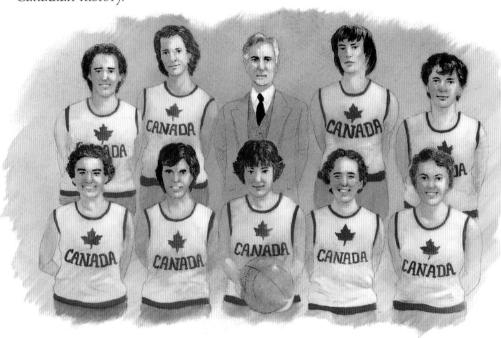

Catriona LeMay Doan

At the 2002 Olympic Winter Games, Catriona LeMay Doan struck gold in speed skating, just as she had at the 1998 Olympics. That made her the first Canadian individual to win gold twice in a row. But she had a bumpy journey getting there.

When Catriona was ten, she and her sister saw a speed-skating ad and decided to try the sport. As soon as Catriona began competing she started winning. It wasn't long before all the skaters in her age group got so frustrated that they

quit. She was just too tough to beat.

However, at the 1992 Olympics, Catriona placed no higher than 14th in the five events she entered. The 1996 Olympics were worse: she crashed and fell. That disaster forced her to rethink her focus and her training. "I think I'm a better athlete now because of that fall," Catriona says. "I'm stronger in every way."

Catriona set records in both the 1000 metre race and the 500 metre. She held eight consecutive world records for the shorter distance, something no other woman has done.

MORE GREAT CANADIAN WOMEN

Canadian women have succeeded in many areas of achievement and in many countries, not just Canada. Here are 29 more great Canadian women, ranging from judges and journalists to comedians and composers, singers and scientists.

Rosalie Abella (1946–)  became the youngest judge in Canada when she was appointed to the Ontario Family Court in 1976 — she was just 29. In 2004 she became a judge on the Supreme Court of Canada, the country's top court. Rosalie is known as a human-rights expert and for encouraging women to choose law as a career.

Molly Brant (1736–1796)  was one of the most important women in North American Aboriginal history. A Mohawk, she was head of the Six Nations matrons, a powerful group of women who chose the chiefs of the Iroquois Confederacy (government). The Mohawk people consulted Molly on all major decisions.

Kim Campbell (1947–) was Canada's first woman prime minister, holding the position from June 25, 1993, to November 4, 1993. Other firsts in Kim's political career include being Canada's first female Minister of Justice and Attorney General in 1990, first female Minister of National Defence in 1993 and first woman leader of the Progressive Conservative party.

Kit Coleman (1864–1915) reported from Cuba on the Spanish-American War in 1898, becoming the world's first female war correspondent. Also the first woman to be in charge of her own section in a Canadian newspaper (*The Mail*), she wrote about politics, fashion and more. Kit was outspoken and had many fans — including Prime Minister Wilfrid Laurier.

Carrie Best (1903–2001) published the *Clarion*, a newspaper especially for Black people in Nova Scotia. The paper was started in 1946, and later that year Carrie used it to publicize the discrimination that Viola Desmond (page 11) was fighting. Energetic and courageous, Carrie won many awards for her activism.

June Callwood (1924–) is famous not only for her award-winning work as a journalist but also as a social activist. She has helped homeless youth and drug addicts find the assistance they need and also started Toronto's Casey House, the world's first hospice (care home) for people dying of AIDS.

Charmaine Crooks (1962–) is the first Canadian women to run 800 metres in less than two minutes. She has won many medals, including silver at the 1984 Olympic Games.

Amelia Douglas (1812–1890) was just 16 when attackers raided the trading fort where her husband, James, was in charge. They threatened to kill him, but Amelia used her knowledge of Aboriginal customs (her mother was Cree) to send them away. James was made governor of today's British Columbia in 1858, and Amelia became famous for helping the poor and sick.

Moira Dunbar (1918–1999)  pioneered Arctic sea-ice research. She was the first woman to make scientific observations from Canadian icebreakers and one of the first women to fly over the North Pole. Moira overcame people's prejudices against having a woman on military planes and ships and became an expert on sea ice.

Barbara Frum (1937–1992) won many journalism awards for her work on radio and TV. She was one of Canada's best-known broadcasters and was famous for her straightforward style of interviewing both celebrities and ordinary people from around the world.

Grace Hartman (1918–1993) 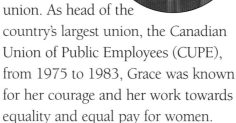 was the first woman to be president of a Canadian labour union. As head of the country's largest union, the Canadian Union of Public Employees (CUPE), from 1975 to 1983, Grace was known for her courage and her work towards equality and equal pay for women.

Monica Hughes (1925–2003) is loved by kids around the world for the books she wrote, especially for her science-fiction. Her best-known books include the Isis series, *Devil on My Back* and *The Crystal Drop*. Overpopulation, dependence on technology and the importance of feelings and knowing yourself are some of the subjects Monica tackled in her books.

Lynn Johnston (1947–) created 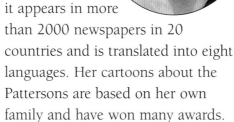 the comic strip *For Better or Worse* in 1979, and now it appears in more than 2000 newspapers in 20 countries and is translated into eight languages. Her cartoons about the Pattersons are based on her own family and have won many awards.

Alexina Louie (1949–) is one of Canada's most famous composers. In her music you can hear the influences of her Chinese heritage blend with those from Canada. Alexina has written music for movies, as well as an opera, but is best known for her music for orchestras.

Flora MacDonald (1926–) became Canada's Secretary of State for External Affairs in 1979. That made her the first Canadian woman to have such an important job in the Cabinet. Flora was a Member of Parliament from 1972 to 1988 and has been outspoken on topics ranging from the Constitution and jails to the environment in poorer countries of the world.

Clara Brett Martin (1874–1923) became the first woman lawyer not only in Canada but in the whole British Empire. She succeeded in 1897 only after she had challenged and changed the laws that prevented women from studying law. Despite a very successful career as a lawyer, Clara rarely appeared in court because her presence caused such a commotion.

Beverley McLachlin (1943–) became the first female Chief Justice of Canada on January 7, 2000. That means she is the top judge in the Supreme Court, the country's highest court. Beverley has a reputation for being down-to-earth, not being swayed by other people's opinions and speaking out on issues such as free speech.

Joni Mitchell (1943–) began studying classical piano when she was seven but today is known for her unique guitar style, breezy voice and moving song lyrics. Joni has won numerous awards and has influenced many singers, including Sarah McLachlan and Diana Krall (page 23).

Anne Murray (1945–) was the first Canadian woman performer to record a song that sold more than 1 million copies. The song "Snowbird" made her a star across North America. Thanks to her rich, friendly voice and her ability to sing many different styles of songs, Anne has won numerous awards.

Olivia Poole (1889–1975) invented the Jolly Jumper in 1948. This hanging seat allows babies to bounce and strengthen their leg muscles while also amusing themselves. To create the Jolly Jumper, Olivia combined modern technology with a traditional Aboriginal design. Her creation is one of the world's most famous inventions for babies.

Mary Pratt (1935–) gave up painting in the early 1960s when her children were young. She went back to her art a few years later and began painting things she found around the house, such as fruit bowls, lunch boxes and even dirty dishes. Mary became famous for these works, especially because of the strong sense of detail, colour and light she brings to them.

Shawnadithit (1801–1829)  was the last of the Beothuk, a group of Aboriginal people who lived in Newfoundland. Most of what is known about the Beothuk comes from the information about their language and customs that Shawnadithit recorded before she died and the sketches that she made.

Corrine Sparks (1954–) became Canada's first Black woman judge when she was appointed to the Nova Scotia Family Court in 1987. She was also the first Black Nova Scotian judge on the Provincial Court of Nova Scotia.

Kateri Tekakwitha (1656–1680) performed many good deeds despite being visually impaired due to smallpox. In 1980 she became the first Aboriginal person in North America to be declared "blessed" by the Catholic church. That means she may someday become Saint Kateri.

Anne Underhill (1920 – 2003) was one of the first Canadian women astrophysicists (scientists who study the physics of stars and other objects in space). She investigated how stars are born, and studied the winds that flow from stars. As a top researcher at NASA, Anne helped develop satellites to observe stars and planets.

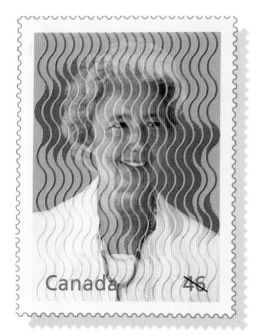

Lucille Teasdale (1929–1996) was the first woman in Quebec to become a surgeon. From 1961 to 1996, she and her husband worked in Uganda, caring for patients in the midst of poverty, epidemics and war. In 1986 Lucille and her husband were awarded the Sasakawa Prize, the highest award given by the World Health Organization of the United Nations.

Thanadelthur (?–1717) was a Chipewyan translator and mediator who is famous for bringing peace between her people and the Cree people in the area that is now Manitoba. Because of her intelligence and knowledge of languages, Thanadelthur was also very helpful to Hudson's Bay Company fur traders in the early 1700s.

Mary Walsh (1952–) created one of Canada's most popular comedy shows, *This Hour Has 22 Minutes*, in 1992. With her distinctly Newfoundland style of humour, Mary has starred in plays, television shows and movies and has won many awards for her work. She especially enjoys poking fun at politicians.

Sharon Wood (1957–) was the first North American woman to reach the summit of Mount Everest, on May 20, 1986. Sharon continues to climb some of the most difficult peaks on Earth and teaches mountain climbing.

Time Line

Great Canadian Women	Date	Canadian Events
	1500	
	1535	Canada gets its name from Huron-Iroquois word for settlement, *Kanata*
Marie de La Tour (1602–1645) (p. 11)	**1600**	
Jeanne Mance (1606–1673) (p. 8)	1605	Port-Royal built by French
	1608	Quebec city founded
	1642	Ville-Marie (today's Montreal) founded
Kateri Tekakwitha (1656–1680) (p. 61)	**1650**	
Madeleine de Verchères (1678–1747) (p. 9)	1670	Hudson's Bay Company founded
Thanadelthur (?–1717) (p. 61)		
Molly Brant (1736–1796) (p. 58)	**1700**	
Elizabeth Simcoe (1762–1850) (p. 32)	**1750**	
Laura Secord (1775–1868) (p. 7)	1755	Expulsion of Acadians
James Barry (1795–1865) (p. 36)	1759	Battle of Plains of Abraham
	1791	Constitutional Act creates Upper and Lower Canada
Shawnadithit (1801–1829) (p. 60)	**1800**	
Catharine Parr Traill (1802–1899) (p. 44)	1812	Red River Settlement begun
Susanna Moodie (1803–1885) (p. 44)	1812–1814	War of 1812
Amelia Douglas (1812–1890) (p. 59)	1830s–60s	Underground Railroad
Harriet Tubman (1820–1913) (p. 8)	1837–38	Rebellions in Lower and Upper Canada
Mary Ann Shadd (1823–1893) (p. 12)	1841	Upper and Lower Canada are joined to create Province of Canada
Emily Stowe (1831–1903) (p. 37)		
Catherine Schubert (1835–1918) (p. 26)		
Frances Ann Hopkins (1838–1919) (p. 29)		
Emma Albani (1847–1930) (p. 22)		
Henrietta Muir Edwards (1849–1931) (p. 6)		
Leonora King (1851–1925) (p. 38)	**1850**	
Faith Fenton (1857–1936) (p. 25)	1858	Fraser River gold rush begins
Adelaide Hoodless (1857–1910) (p. 16)	1862	Overlanders travel from Ontario to British Columbia
Ishbel Gordon (1857–1939) (p. 16)	1867	Dominion of Canada formed with provinces of New Brunswick, Nova Scotia, Ontario and Quebec
Armine Gosling (1861–1942) (p. 9)		
Ella Cora Hind (1861–1942) (p. 43)	1869–70	Red River Rebellion
Pauline Johnson (1861–1913) (p. 42)	1870	Hudson's Bay Company sells its territory to Canada
Mary Schäffer Warren (1861–1939) (p. 27)		Manitoba becomes Canada's fifth province
Georgina Pope (1862–1938) (p. 10)	1871	British Columbia becomes Canada's sixth province
Kit Coleman (1864–1915) (p. 58)	1873	Prince Edward Island becomes Canada's seventh province
Martha Black (1866–1957) (p. 27)	1874	The North West Mounted Police made official police force in Canadian west
Louise McKinney (1868–1931) (p. 6)	1878	Woman's Medical College opens in Toronto
Emily Murphy (1868–1933) (p. 6)	1885	Northwest Rebellion
Irene Parlby (1868–1965) (p. 6)		Canadian Pacific Railway completed
Maude Abbott (1869–1940) (p. 34)	1893	National Council of Women of Canada founded
Mina Hubbard (1870–1956) (p. 26)	1897	Victorian Order of Nurses formed
Emily Carr (1871–1945) (p. 28)		Women's Institute founded
Nellie McClung (1873–1951) (p. 6)	1897–99	Klondike gold rush
Clara Brett Martin (1874–1923) (p. 60)	1898	Yukon Territory created
Lucy Maud Montgomery (1874–1942) (p. 40)	1899–1902	South African (Boer) War
Harriet Brooks Pitcher (1876–1933) (p. 35)		
Frances McGill (1882–1959) (p. 37)		
Elizabeth Arden (1878–1966) (p. 13)		
Helen McNicoll (1879–1915) (p. 30)		
Alice Wilson (1881–1964) (p. 39)		
Florence Wyle (1881–1968) (p. 32)		
Cairine Wilson (1885–1962) (p. 48)		
Frances Loring (1887–1968) (p. 32)		
Margaret "Ma" Murray (1888–1982) (p. 41)		
Olivia Poole (1889–1975) (p. 60)		
Agnes Macphail (1890–1954) (p. 47)		
Kate Aitken (1891–1971) (p. 15)		
Mary Pickford (1892–1979) (p. 19)		
Phyllis Munday (1894–1990) (p. 25)		
Thérèse Casgrain (1896–1981) (p. 49)		
Paraskeva Clark (1898–1986) (p. 33)		
Carrie Best (1903–2001) (p. 58)	**1900**	
Maud Lewis (1903–1970) (p. 31)	1905	Alberta and Saskatchewan become provinces
Viola MacMillan (1903–1993) (p. 13)	1910	Girl Guides begin in Canada
Pitseolak Ashoona (1904–1983) (p. 30)	1914–18	World War I

Madeleine de Verchères

Lucy Maud Montgomery

1916	Women get the vote in Manitoba, Saskatchewan and Alberta
1917	Women get the vote in British Columbia and Ontario
1918	Women get the vote in federal elections
	Women get the vote in Nova Scotia
1919	Women get the vote in New Brunswick and Yukon Territory
1922	Women get the vote in Prince Edward Island
1925	Women get the vote in Newfoundland and Labrador
1929	Persons Case won by Famous Five
1929–39	Great Depression
1939	Canadian Elizabeth Fry Society founded
1939–45	World War II
1940	Women get the vote in Quebec

Marilyn Bell

1950	
1951	Women get the vote in Northwest Territories (Nunavut was part of the Northwest Territories until 1999)
1956	Law passed to guarantee Canadian women are paid the same as men for the same work
1965	Canada gets its Maple Leaf flag
1966	Medical Care Act (medicare) passed
1967	Canada's Centennial year
	Royal Commission on the Status of Women formed
1969	Official Languages Act passed
1970	Canadian Advisory Council on the Status of Women formed
	The October Crisis
1972	National Action Committee on the Status of Women founded
1976	Parti Québécois elected in Quebec
1982	The Charter of Rights and Freedoms and Constitution Act become law
1992	Canada chooses October for celebrating Women's History Month
1999	New territory of Nunavut is formed
2000	Clarity Bill describes terms of Quebec's separation
2001	*Canadarm2* attached to International Space Station
2002	Canada signs the Kyoto Protocol to reduce greenhouse gases

Index